Thanksgiving Tales

Thanksgiving Tales

True Stories of the Holiday in America

EDITED BY BRIAN D. JAFFE

Sestin LLC
NEW YORK, NY

First edition, 2010

Published by Sestin LLC
New York, NY
www.sestinllc.com

For further information, including inquiries for permission to reproduce,
go to www.sestinllc.com or e-mail info@sestinllc.com

Library of Congress Control Number: 2010907770
ISBN 978-0-9827290-0-7

Cover and text design by John Reinhardt Book Design

Printed in the United States of America.

For Ann and Marc

Contents

Preface

THANKSGIVING is a different kind of holiday. While other U.S. holidays honor individuals (e.g., President's Day, Martin Luther King Jr. Day), events (e.g., Independence Day), or groups (e.g., Veteran's Day, Memorial Day), Thanksgiving is more associated with an idea or concept... giving thanks.

In the national archives you can learn that the first official national observance of Thanksgiving was on November 26, 1789, as defined in a proclamation from President George Washington.[1]

President Abraham Lincoln, in 1863, issued a Presidential Proclamation for Thanksgiving to be observed on the last Thursday in November. In 1939, President Franklin D. Roosevelt signed a Presidential Proclamation moving the holiday to the second-to-last Thursday of November (apparently in response to retailers wanting to start the holiday shopping season a week earlier), although some states continued to celebrate on the last Thursday of the month.

Finally, in 1941, Congress passed, and Roosevelt signed, a resolution establishing the fourth Thursday as the national Thanksgiving Holiday.

By far, Thanksgiving is my favorite holiday. There is really nothing to dislike about this holiday—no one expects a greeting card or gift; and everything to love about it—as a national holiday it's a day off

[1] http://www.archives.gov/legislative/features/thanksgiving/

from work (and thanks to Washington, Lincoln, and countless members of Congress, it's on a Thursday, giving many a four-day weekend), and the entire holiday is centered around a large meal with family and friends.

I don't know a lot about Thanksgiving. Oh sure, I remember being taught about the first Thanksgiving in grade school, I've seen Norman Rockwell paintings, and as a kid, I went to the Macy's parade in New York City. But, in truth, my own Thanksgiving experience is pretty limited.

I've never been to a Thanksgiving outside of my own family. All my Thanksgivings have been hosted either in the house I grew up in, or within 25 miles of it, and always in the home of a family member. I'm not sure we've ever had a Thanksgiving meal with less than three generations around the table, and there were many with four generations.

Of the past 25 Thanksgivings, 24 have been hosted by Marc and Ann, my brother and his wife. I distinctly remember the first Thanksgiving they hosted, and their near-panic that the turkey's pop-up timer wasn't popping, and the way they hugged each other when it finally did. Now, 25 years later, they are seasoned veterans. A last-minute guest? No problem, there's always plenty of food and a way to squeeze in another chair at the table. Special dietary requirements? They'll have something ready just for you.

In our family, Thanksgiving is about a six-hour affair and considerably longer for Ann and Marc. In the past few years, we've been numbering about 15–20 in attendance. We gather in the mid-afternoon to start chatting, nibbling on snacks, watching TV, enjoying the fireplace, and helping Ann and Marc wherever needed. Then there is the meal (fairly traditional... turkey, stuffing, potatoes, vegetables, Mom's cranberry relish, apple cider, pies, Cozmo the dog sniffing around for scraps, etc.), followed by a respite before dessert, and then pitching in to help clean up. When I had been dating my wife, Jenine, for about three months, I had thought about asking her to join us at Thanksgiving, but decided against it. It would've been the first time she was introduced to any of my family, and it just seemed that such a long event, and meeting so many people, might be overwhelming. She understood my decision when she joined us at the Thanksgiving table the following year, and every year since.

I have a hard time distinguishing one Thanksgiving from another. Oh sure, there were some with rain, some with snow, the one with the butternut squash soup, the first one with the renovated kitchen, etc. But the real differences are more subtle from year to year... watching the kids grow while some of the adults get a little grayer, seeing new additions to the head-count around the table, and remembering those no longer with us.

As you can see from the stories that follow, Thanksgiving holds a special place in the minds of Americans. It is a holiday for everyone, whether your family came here via the Mayflower, Ellis Island, international airport, or any other way. It is a holiday steeped in traditions (which are either faithfully followed, radically ignored, or adapted to individual circumstances), memories and images.

These stories describe Thanksgivings of very varied types, from those that will make you laugh, to those that evoke more serious emotions, and those that just may make you stop, think, and remember. But, there is a unifying theme. It doesn't matter what food is served, how it's made, or where the meal is held. What matters is how you spend the day and who you spend it with—the same wisdom I learned at an early age from my mother and father. I hope you enjoy these stories as much as I've enjoyed reading them and assembling this collection.

Obviously, this book would not be possible without the contributions of the writers, and I am grateful to them for sharing their treasured memories, stories and emotions. I must also thank my sister, Suzanne, for her support and assistance with this project, and throughout life; and to my love, my wife Jenine, for her unwavering patience, support and understanding.

BRIAN D. JAFFE
Editor
brian@sestinllc.com

CAROLE McCRACKEN

Cranberry Sauce!

TO ME, Thanksgiving means watching the Macy's Day Parade on television, the smell of cooked turkey throughout my house, and cranberry sauce! When my daughter was five years old, I started a tradition that I've carried out for 30 years and plan to continue for years to come! I made cranberry sauce from fresh cranberries. Until that day, our Thanksgiving table had a bowl of cranberry sauce that came out of a can.

When my little girl was in kindergarten, her teacher sent her home with a recipe that called for a bag of fresh cranberries, a cup of water, a teaspoon of orange juice and a cup of sugar. Before then, I had no idea that I could buy fresh cranberries in a bag. I thought I'd try the grocery store and see if they were sold there. Who knew that an ordinary grocery store sold a bag of fresh cranberries? Surprisingly, I found a bag in, of all places, the cranberry section in the grocery store. I came home, opened the bag, poured the cranberries and the other ingredients into a medium-sized pot, and my little kindergartener and I stirred for quite awhile until the cranberries softened and looked mushy! The texture certainly didn't compare with our

---

My name is Carole McCracken. I am excited to write about the Thanksgiving tradition in my home! I hope you enjoy learning about my tradition, and I hope my children will carry it on even after I am gone. Feel free to email me at CaroleJMcCracken@yahoo.com.

beloved jellied cranberry sauce in a can, but my child was happy, so I was happy, too.

When it came time to put all the Thanksgiving fare on the table, my little girl and I proudly placed the bowl of our freshly cooked cranberry sauce alongside the good old standby from the can. I'm sure the meal was delicious, but the only thing I remember about it now is that I had to force myself to eat mushy cranberry sauce with some cranberry bits in it, when I really wanted the jellied stuff out of the can. I don't remember which one my daughter chose, but I know there was a lot of our cooked cranberry sauce left over, while the canned cranberry sauce disappeared in no time. After the table was cleared, the cooked cranberry sauce was covered and refrigerated. It stayed in the refrigerator until it looked like a science project. Then it went into the trash. I did not let that stop me from making it the next year and the year after that.

Every Thanksgiving, I still make cranberry sauce from fresh cranberries, using the recipe that my little girl brought home from kindergarten. My little girl is now 35 years old, and I wouldn't dream of not making that dish. It's become our Thanksgiving tradition and when we have company at our Thanksgiving table, we are quick to tell them the story of the recipe brought home by my little girl years ago.

This year, with the advice of a good friend, I put some extra sugar and extra orange juice in the cooked cranberry sauce, and kept adding more sugar until it was as sweet as my little girl! So much has changed in our lives over the past 30 years, a lot good and some not so good. But one thing that we can all count on every year is the tradition of the cooked cranberry sauce and knowing that it all started with the recipe that was brought home by a little five-year-old child!

PATRICIA LAPIDUS

A Musical Thanksgiving

WE WENT OVER the river and through the woods to Grandmother's house, or rather, down the rutted Oak Hill Road and over Litchfield Plains in my father's International Harvester Truck. This was his first vehicle and he wasn't quite used to leaving the horses in the barn.

My older sister Winky and I sat like big girls between our father and mother. (This was way before seat belts were invented.) Our baby sister Meddy sat on Mom's lap. The truck went all of 40 miles an hour. Not much traffic. Most people were at home or had already arrived where they were going for the most special dinner of the year. But Dad had needed to feed his livestock and chickens, to gather the eggs and place them in the cool cellar under our house.

He pulled the truck up behind other cars and trucks along the dirt road and grabbed the baby while Mom took the box of apple and mince pies she had made. "Winky, take Trishy's hand," Mom said. Dutifully, Winky reached and caught my hand, pulling me into the driveway and toward the piazza. I would have headed for the barn where Grampa kept sheep and great big sow pigs and where,

---

Patricia Lapidus has published a memoir of life among spiritual hippies, Sweet Potato Suppers: A Yankee Woman Finds Salvation in a Hippie Village, second edition, *spring 2010.* Swamp Walking Woman, a modern mythic fairy tale, *was published in April 2010.* Red Hen's Daughters, *a collection of poems, was published in 2009.*

only last week, I had been allowed to watch the dressing out of the deer brought home by the hunters. The uncles and any aunts who didn't have too many small children to leave with Grammie all went hunting the week before Thanksgiving. I had imitated my big boy cousins, grabbing two deer legs and running around pretending to be deer.

Winky towed me up the piazza steps and into Grammie's warm kitchen that smelled of roasting chickens and homemade cranberry sauce. As soon as I had my coat off, Grampa grabbed me up. Chanting "Grampa's girl! Grampa's girl!" he tossed me over his head. Unwilling to be thrown away, I grabbed for his salt-and-pepper hair.

My uncles, by setting boards on sawhorses through the archway that connected the dining room with the living room, created one long table with capacity for more than 30 people. My aunts covered the table with cloths and set places. Grampa said, "Trishy sits by me."

I don't know how the special friendship with my grandfather began. I only remember crawling across Grammie's kitchen floor to greet him, the smooth, worn linoleum under my pattering hands. When I reached his boots, he welcomed me always with the same toss over his head, the same, "Grampa's girl! Grampa's girl!" How to explain such an early memory? It must have been the love. I was the middle sister. Winky had the security of her place as first born. As the baby, Meddy was adored. I was hungry for love and my grandfather had a big heart! To me, Grampa was the reason for Thanksgiving.

So I sat on a telephone book in a chair near the head of the table where Grampa reigned. He cut my chicken, spooned up stuffing. I was soon done eating, but Grampa kept me at the table by pulling me onto his lap while he finished off a piece of mince pie, made with fresh ground venison. "Hilda, you make pie like your mother does," he said. My mother smiled shyly, not used to compliments. Because she was a younger sister, Mom had had to watch to learn to cook, hanging out at Grammie and Aunt Freda's elbows or spying on them from the doorway when sent out of the kitchen.

Grampa sent me off to play. While the aunts did the dishes—this was the 1940s and they were not self-conscious in the least about the division of labor—the uncles got out musical instruments. I stopped playing and crept near to see the big cello, the guitars, a trumpet being tuned up. Of course, there was always the piano with Grammie as pianist as soon as the kitchen was cleaned up. Mom tuned up her fiddle. Those that didn't play, sang. And how those folks could sing! They sang hymns and Maine Country music. Using *The Golden Song Book*, they sang songs from the gay 90s and songs from the roaring 20s. They sang "Swing Low, Sweet Chariot" and Stephen Foster's "Beautiful Dreamer." Grammie touched the piano keys with a confidence born of years of playing for church. She sang along while Grampa, standing in the doorway, watched her with fond eyes. "The Old Rugged Cross" and "Shall We Gather at the River" were followed by "Some Little Bug'll Get You Someday," a song whose verses humorously took up the many ways to get ill and die.

My dad would put on a performance, singing by heart all the verses of "Abdullah Bulbul Ameer," a tale of love and treachery set in old Russia. He'd follow it with the story of Johnny Sands, who found a way to be rid of a nagging wife in the days when marriage was final.

As the afternoon mellowed, the musicians went for slower tunes: "I Wandered Today by the Mill, Maggie," "Believe Me if All Those Endearing Young Charms," "When Irish Eyes Are Smiling," and everyone's favorite, "With Someone Like You." These songs followed me into my dreams and formed much of my child view of life.

"With someone like you, a pal good and true,
I'd like to leave it all behind and go and find
A place that's known to God alone,
Just a place to call our own.

We'll find perfect peace where joys never cease
Out there beneath the kindly skies.
We'll build a sweet little nest somewhere in the west
And let the rest of the world go by."

What made the sentiment of the song so believable was the harmony of the family voices. They sang like birds. They sang soprano and alto, tenor, baritone and bass. We were not the only ones who thought "With Someone Like You" was special. Many years later, it was the theme song for the movie *Out of Africa*. There was a time when it seemed one could find a spot and live happy, and "let the rest of the world go by."

Each Thanksgiving, the story is told that when my charming uncles were practicing the wedding march for my parents' nuptials, whenever my mother walked into the room, they switched to, "The Fight Is On," a rousing hymn about the fight to save souls, intended by these rascals to be a tease. It worked. Mom giggled.

The music of Thanksgiving Day wove a culture of safety, an idea that Grampa and the clan were in control of life and would see to it that our dreams came true. Today at Thanksgiving Dinner, I close my eyes and I'm there again, leaning against the boot box with its hinged seat smoothed by the posteriors of the family men who sat to pull on their boots, short beside the tall boot box back with pegs holding coats, above the back *way high*, a shelf keeping hats. I am leaning on one of the curved sides of the boot box and listening while Uncle Chester raises a trumpet up to the tune of "When the Saints Go Marching In," and Uncle Granville, drawing a lively bow across the cello, sings along. The joined voices become one voice that says, "We are a family, we are the folks."

TERRI ELDERS

Spellbound by Swanky Swigs

THIS PAST NOVEMBER, I laid in a good supply of cheese spreads...for stuffing celery for Thanksgiving dinner, of course. My grocer still stocks those little Kraft jars with the savory olive pimiento and roka blue flavors I've always loved, but I regret that now they're sold in plain little glass jars, not the glamorous red tulip or blue cornflower juice glasses of my girlhood. Even so, I could hardly wait to get the jars home and once again sample my favorite canapé.

Of course, if they were still around, Grandma and Mama probably would laugh at my nostalgia, just as they laughed at those glasses in their 1940s heyday, and at Auntie Dorothy who always toted them to our holiday feast. Even as a girl, I realized that when it came to holiday dinners, my female forbears were culinary elitists with rigid ideas about appropriate bills of fare. Cheese-stuffed celery, in their view, was just plain cheesy. And Grandma and Mama could be downright catty.

Terri Elders' stories appear in multiple anthologies, including Chicken Soup for the Soul, A Cup of Comfort, HCI Ultimate, *and Literary Cottage's Hero series. She lives near Colville, WA, with two dogs and three cats. She is a public member of the Washington Medical Commission. You can write to her at telders@hotmail.com.*

Looking back it seems as if every year, as soon as we set aside the candy corn and *jack-o'-lanterns,* Grandma and Mama would huddle in the kitchen to conduct their annual Thanksgiving dinner debate.

One year when I was twelve, the awkward age, too old for toys, too young for boys, I joined the women in the kitchen, volunteering to peel potatoes or shell peas. I had seen Grandma pull her writing tablet and yellow pencil out of her purse, and knew that the confab was about to begin. The two would bicker and banter on the venue and the menu…and then get down to the real family gossip as they discussed who would bring what. I didn't want to miss a word.

"We'll do it again at my house, since I have the larger dining room," Grandma began.

"But our house is so much more accessible," Mama countered.

"I have a kitchen table for the children," Grandma parried.

I smiled to myself. Grandma always won this argument. Never in my memory had the family gathered elsewhere, but Mama always felt obligated to put in her pitch. I'd overheard her tell Daddy she didn't know how she'd accommodate everybody if Grandma ever actually gave in.

"I've been thinking about the menu. Maybe a ham would be nice this year," Mama ventured, winking at me. I knew she loved to tease Grandma.

"Oh, Mama, that sounds wonderful, and with pineapple garnishes!" I chimed in, conspiratorially.

"For heaven's sake, it's Thanksgiving. We'll have turkey just as we always do," Grandma folded her arms and stared at the two of us as if we'd both lost our senses.

Mama nodded. "Ok, I'll bake the pumpkin pies."

"And I'll make lemon meringue, since you know that the boys don't like pumpkin."

Grandma tapped her pencil on the table. "Should we ask Joe and Julia if they'd do the sweet potatoes and mashed potatoes? Joe always eats three times more potatoes than everybody else put together, so maybe if they're in charge they'll bring enough to go around."

Mama and I grinned. Burly Uncle Joe could be counted on to ensure there'd be no leftover spuds. When he'd ask for his fourth helping, Aunt Julia would pass him the bowl with a big smile, proud of her trencherman spouse.

"And what about Teddy?" Mama loved her bachelor stepbrother, but she knew he couldn't cook worth a whit.

"Let's ask him to bring some wine," Grandma said, gnawing on her pencil. "He makes plenty of dough, so maybe we should suggest champagne."

Mama brightened. I don't think I'd ever seen champagne at a family feast, and I don't recall Mama and Daddy having any even on New Year's Eve.

"Poor Opal can bring the green bean casserole," Grandma continued. I perked up, waiting for more information. It was true that Auntie Opal always looked pale and tired, but I wasn't certain why.

"Well, the way Jim drinks, Opal has to look after the house, the jewelry shop *and* raise those kids practically on her own. It'll be a wonder if she finds the energy to open a can of onion rings," Mama observed.

Grandma stared at her tablet and scribbled a few words. "I'll do the turkey, stuffing and gravy, and you can make some rolls. I guess Dorothy will bring the celery," Grandma said, looking up. "And she'll think she's done something special when she brings that dreadful processed cheese in those dinky little glasses."

Mama snickered, but I held my breath. I loved helping Auntie Dorothy stuff the celery, and I adored the elegant flowered glasses she said were mine.

Mama sighed. "Just because she and Roy never had children is no reason for her not to learn to cook. She should be making decent suppers for her husband instead of expecting him to live on baked beans and bacon sandwiches."

I set down my potato peeler and waited expectantly. I couldn't imagine Daddy's reaction if Mama put such a meal before him, but it sure sounded tasty to me.

"Roy has the patience of a saint," Grandma said, shaking her head. "Imagine that woman off to the church every day to play the piano for choir practice, when she should be cleaning that little apartment." I'd been to those practices with Auntie Dorothy. The choir even let me sing along, even though I knew I wasn't quite on pitch.

On Thanksgiving we gathered at Grandma's. Uncle Jim greeted us jovially, smelling of equal parts Old Spice and Old Crow. Uncle Joe huffed and puffed up the steps, a tub of potatoes tucked under each arm. When Auntie Dorothy arrived with her big brown bag, I hurried to her side.

"Can I help you get your celery ready?"

"Of course, and I've got another cheese glass for you, too." I gaped, spellbound, as she pulled the latest acquisition to my collection out of the bag... a rare black tulip.

Today I open my kitchen cabinet and gaze at the miniature tumblers that I've treasured for over half a century: tulips, forget-me-nots, lilies of the valley, bachelor buttons, and my favorite, a light blue cornflower with emerald leaves.

When I checked recently on e-Bay, I was astonished to learn that these days collectors call these humble glasses *swanky swigs*, and they're highly regarded for their ornate decals. They now sell for what Grandma would have called a pretty penny. Why, one set of four blue tulips is listed for 20 bucks, and forget-me-nots go for at least eight dollars each.

I pull down the black tulip and hold it up to the sunlight. Not only can I recall the snap and crunch of Auntie Dorothy's celery filled with pineapple cheese, I remember how Mama poured half an inch of Teddy's bubbly into this very same tumbler, and I, feeling swanky indeed, had taken my first swig of champagne.

For supper tonight maybe I'll fry up some bacon and open a can of beans, fill a few stalks of celery with roka blue. I'll check the pantry for champagne, so I can toast to the entire family that provided such memorable Thanksgiving dinners, including, especially, Auntie Dorothy.

JOHN McCLUSKEY

This Moment

The guests are all accounted for,
the house can clearly hold no more,
but just before we sit to eat
there's one last chore I must complete.

I step outside to gather wood
and stay much longer than I should.
Though wood will burn throughout our meal,
this moment has its own appeal,

which I believe with certitude
has all along been solitude -
to gather wood is to commune
with late November afternoon.

So when it's time to feed the fire,
may gratitude these logs inspire.
Return me then to family feast
with blessed wood, with grace, with peace.

John McCluskey has published poetry, fiction, and non-fiction in literary and commercial publications. He recently obtained a Master of Arts in Writing (MAW) from Manhattanville College, Purchase, NY. John has lived in Chicago and Los Angeles before settling in Connecticut. He is currently working on his second novel.

RACHEL WILKERSON

Oh, Stuff It!

THE IDEA OF A HAPPY FAMILY dressed in lovely sweaters, gathering around a steaming, equally well-dressed turkey and raising a wine glass to how much they love each other, has been a fantasy of mine for years. At this point, it looks like I am going to have to get married to said family and start reproducing perfect children of my own, so I can have that holiday.

It usually goes like this: my grandma works on holidays (she's a nurse, so she can make mad overtime, and we're all old enough to not really mind), so my mother does the cooking. My mother doesn't eat anything all day because she's too busy, plus she forgot to buy real groceries when she bought all the other groceries, so there's not enough food (or time) to make a damn sandwich. Plus, if it's Christmas, she's going on about three hours of sleep, due to a late night of wrapping. She's trying to cook all by herself all in one day to get ready for a ridiculous eating time of 3:00 in the afternoon, and she's got my five-year-old brother Preston to entertain, and, well, the kid's a "before" in an ADHD medication ad.

So my mom is in the kitchen, sweating bullets because the oven has raised the temperature in the house 15 degrees, but icy blasts from the open window are making me cold. By noon, three arguments

---

Rachel Wilkerson graduated from Michigan State University, where she wrote the sexy sorority blog, The Spartanette. *She is now a freelance writer and social media consultant, and the creator and author of the blog,* Shedding It & Getting It.

over the open window have already taken place. Then my grandma comes home from work around 15 minutes before we're supposed to eat, and asks something innocent like, "Did you make the mashed potatoes yet?" At this, my mom blows up about why she didn't make the mashed potatoes ("First I had to go out for BUTTER, and then Preston BROKE THE DVD PLAYER, and I still have to take a SHOWER...") and my grandma snaps back, and the bitch-fest just takes off. Five minutes later, my aunt and uncle show up with their kids, and so then there are kids running everywhere, meaning there's more bitching—first at the children, and then at the parents. Then the uncle everyone hates shows up. (He's legitimately hated; just last month he declared bankruptcy after buying new veneers for a crack whore.) This uncle is followed by my other uncle who happens to be gay, but also happens to drive a semi-truck and live in a house decorated in all types of Confederacy memorabilia. Things get even more tense and awkward, plus now the dog is barking, so everyone's screaming at the dog, and each other, and our house and kitchen is just too small, and the fact of the matter is, no one in my family drinks (except for me, obviously), so everyone's just PISSED.

And meanwhile, there's me, usually just chilling on the couch, reading or browsing the Internet, and not flipping out, 'cause, well, it's a holiday and I'd prefer not to go there. Mainly, I'm just trying to distract myself from thoughts of how many carbs I'm about to consume, carbs I don't even like all that much. Sometimes I can't resist taking a shot at my mom's poor time-management skills, and then more bitching ensues, but I find it worth it. Eventually, I just start drinking alone at this point, 'cause it's just the only way to deal.

If my mom and I venture to the *other* side of the family's house for a holiday (my dad's family), at 4:00 P.M., the relative who was supposed to be doing the grocery shopping will have not returned from the grocery store yet, because the fact is, old-school black people are just not timely (YUP). By 7:00 P.M., *maybe* the turkey will have gone in the oven, but definitely no one's made the mac-and-cheese yet. If at 10:00 P.M. my mom gets a little impatient, because, you know, her three-year-old daughter should be in bed, she's "disrespectful" (and, well, *white*), so she bites her tongue and doesn't say anything when we eat at midnight.

When I do the cooking, which is more and more often these days, I don't allow anyone to bitch in my kitchen. The actual holiday is pleasant enough, but the week leading up to it is pretty tense. I have to remind my family members that I don't prepare elaborate meals so they can show up in clothes I might wear when I'm washing my dog. I have to let my mom know that Preston cannot bring a noise-making rocket blaster toy to the dinner table. And then there's the argument with my mother over what food I am making and how much food we need. Generally, there is way too much food; my mom's menus aren't well planned and leftovers usually get tossed. It is a waste of food and money, but my mother does not see it this way. "People like leftovers..." It's always "people," as if all these strangers are showing up.

So I try to bite my lip as she says, "Are you going to make...?" or "I picked up some shrimp cocktail in case you want to have that..." or "Did you think about...?" But when she starts telling me to make more food so they can be gluttonous for a week as opposed to just a day, my (clearly inherited) bitchy tone comes out, and I shut her down and remind her that when I've got the apron on, I call the shots, and, ultimately, she can give thanks that all she has to do is show up and eat.

But back at Grandma's, we finally sit down to eat at a not-beautifully set table with no music playing (because no one in my family appreciates this), and everyone is rocking hoodies and elastic-waist pants (because the concept of "dressing for dinner" is a bit lost on my family, even when dinner is a $250 meal). Things are still relatively tense. My grandma will suggest we say grace, and, to be a pain in the ass, I will roll my eyes and take a bite of mashed potatoes before anyone can make the sign of the cross, pointing out that we never go to church or do anything remotely religious *ever*. The food is fine, but relatively boring, because no one in my family likes trying new things, and I'm annoyed at having eaten 1,200 calories of food that I didn't even like that much. Dinner is finished by 5:00 P.M., so no one knows what to do for the rest of the night. At 7:00, we just have to eat leftovers, because now it's actually dinner time and all the white carbs have made us hungry again. And, well, there you have it. Happy Holidays.

BILL CLIFFORD

The Holiday of Holidays

THE HOLIDAY OF HOLIDAYS, the summation of all rejoicing, Thanksgiving! The rewards of sowing, weeding, hoeing and reaping, whether figuratively, or in our case, literally, laid upon the table on The Thursday afternoon. Grain to bread, seed to veggies and the peeping poults to roasting birds, are all prepared to consolidate and celebrate all holidays at once. Mothers, fathers, everyone who had a birthday, the veterans and everything else on the calendar, especially God, are celebrated. There is no other day of the year that crosses all the lines of ideology and reality, profound theology and tangible worldly successes. Prepared, shared and given not to celebrate the bounty, wealth or bragging rights, but shared as an offering to family, friends and God.

Humorously, I have always made light of the day. I laugh and share my thoughts on the day off from work, the reprieve from buying gifts (I have always verbalized my disdain for giving gifts because the calendar dictates) and the requirement to eat too much, drink excessively and enjoy my family and friends. I always plop onto the couch,

---

Bill Clifford, 45, was born in Ft. Lauderdale in 1963. Throughout college he worked in food service and went on to become a successful restauranteur. He mastered his skills as a Mess Specialist in the Navy. Now residing in Greenfield, IN, with his wife Michelle, he gladly prepares Thanksgiving dinner annually for all who come.

watch the game and ask, "Why don't we do this every Thursday?" One could only imagine, Thursdays off to eat and watch football!

Straggling guests always laugh, my family knows better and sees through the humor. I have never been able to get through our asking for the blessing without my eyes welling with tears. Joyful, but tears nonetheless. Nor is it lost on these fine folks that I always plan a roasted bird, a smoked bird and, weather permitting, a deep-fried turkey along with all the basic amenities made from scratch. It is not that I am a martyr who suffers through the preparation; I just like my own cooking and gladly spend countless hours on the project. The pantry and freezer full of the fruits of the garden are represented and prepared for all. Yes, I mean all. Everyone is invited and the guest list is open-ended, standing at 30 plus or minus with contingencies for 10–20 surprise guests. My standing rule is that the best part of Thanksgiving is leftovers. Everyone leaves with a plate to take home. The hugs and smiles are as nurturing as the food itself. The remembering of family members who passed and the excitement of babies expected is constant: only the names change and it feeds the soul more completely than the meal. I love these people, even the ones I had never met before.

Our 105-year-old farmhouse has the room, the parking, and the indifference to abuse that makes it an ideal venue for such a celebration. We have gladly hosted Thanksgiving every year. I selfishly offer to cook for all, provided I am not required to go anywhere and can remain free to drink and watch ball games. I made a mental note of perpetual commitment several years ago when a family member commented that it was so nice that we were all together, and it wasn't for the purpose of burying someone. We have always had plenty. Every year we have cause to give thanks and ample to share. In spite of unemployment, airplane crashes and anything else that could go wrong each year, the show goes on. Thanksgiving gives us an opportunity to see the good, celebrate the overcoming of adversity and have hope for the ensuing year. Sometimes meager and lean, more often decadent and excessive, there has always been enough to fill our home with the foods, aromas, warmth and love that the day intends. Again in 2009, we were able to enjoy the hope and the day unto itself that brings it all together for the opportunity to say, "Thank you."

AMANDA L. CARLSON

The Thanksgiving Wine Whine

THE OVEN DOOR slammed as I crammed the first sheet of rolls into preheated warmth. Flour covered my hands, but I gingerly pressed the oven light on. "What's a little more flour in my already messy kitchen?" I thought to myself, little knowing it was just the beginning.

Despite the hectic kitchen, I couldn't help but notice the quiet of the house. Wiping my hands on a towel, I leaned over my laptop to get some Christmas tunes blaring to quell the silence. Well, since it didn't feel like Thanksgiving, I may as well put on the premature carols.

The morning had been long and lazy: a cup of coffee, a gooey cinnamon roll and an embarrassing amount of time poring over social networking sites. It was officially my first Thanksgiving Day on my own. By "on my own," I mean as a military spouse...with my Air Force husband working the holiday.

The night before, I had sobbed into my pillow that the day would be so long and lonely. My husband assured me that I'd sleep in, get on with my baking and suddenly, the evening would come. I'd load

---

Amanda L. Carlson is a freelance writer and fitness instructor. She currently resides with her husband in Las Vegas, Nevada.

up the car, taking my rolls and pies to the Raihs' for an evening Thanksgiving feast. "The day will fly by," he assured me.

He was right about one thing—it was suddenly time to go, and I flew around the kitchen trying to get everything baked and buttered, chilled and covered. But I had been right about another thing—the day had been lonely.

I had gone jogging around the quiet streets of the neighborhood in the middle of the afternoon. A few people hollered out, "Happy Thanksgiving!" as I ran past, but their looks said, "Who really exercises right after lunch on Thanksgiving anyway?" I huffed and puffed down the sunny streets, thinking about my lonely lot as an Air Force spouse—and this was only Thanksgiving. I still had a lonesome Christmas to anticipate! Glancing up, I noticed a familiar house. The windows were dark, and suddenly, I felt guilty and sad as I remembered the girl who lived there. Her husband was deployed, and I wondered if anyone had asked her to dinner, or if she had gone anywhere. My mind wandered to another lady I knew that was going to a buffet with some of her elderly friends on Thanksgiving Day, even though it was a stretch on her budget. I hadn't even considered them in my self-absorbed pity party. For the first time in my life, my mind wandered to people who really were alone on this holiday. "Do people invite them over, or forget them like I have?" I thought uncomfortably, feeling slightly ashamed of myself.

My husband was working today, but he'd be home tonight. I had wasted an entire morning feeling sorry for myself in a spirit of sensational holiday gloom. I quickened my pace and reached home with new resolve. Today was a day to be thankful for a husband that was working to protect our country and for family and friends that loved me.

Then, as if some little gremlin tried to test that resolve, the hands of the clock spun forward and suddenly I felt pressed for time. The pecan pie, cranberry sauce and sweet tea were ready and waiting, but I still had to roll out the buns and get them baking because it was almost time to go! "Where did my time go?" I wondered with a guilty glance at my laptop on the counter, the ultimate time-waster apparatus!

Racing around the kitchen, trying not to stain my fresh clothes, it happened suddenly. I heard a pop and spun to face the refrigerator from whence the ominous sound erupted. From the top of the fridge, flowing a violent purple stream, came a gushing, unstoppable fountain of wine. The cork had popped out and wine spewed from the bottle's neck. My feet were rooted to the rug.

Realizing that I could perhaps stop the gush, I sprung desperately to reach the top of the fridge to right the bottle, but alas, at five feet and two inches, I was wasting precious time. Grabbing the tallest chair in the house, I set it next to the fridge, stepped up...but, I was too late! The wine was only coming out in jerky little belches—hardly an inch remained in the bottle.

I slowly turned around, bottle in hand, to take in the carnage that was my kitchen. "Bloodbath" came to mind. The wine covered the floor in one giant pool; the walls, rugs and cabinets were splattered with the red juice. The refrigerator dripped ominously—I didn't even want to open it. Of course, at this point, I noticed the rolls turning darker brown while the timer beeped insensitively. In a leap or two, I scaled the large puddle and rescued the rolls while clumsily shoving another sheet of them into the oven.

Then the text messages (from an otherwise silent phone) began flooding in. "Can you bring a glue gun tonight?" "Will you drop something by my house before you leave?" One glance at the oven clock told me I was officially late. The purple grout stared at me, and I knew I'd have to clean it all up before it stained everything in sight. The old feelings of self-pity began creeping back into my chest, and all I wanted to do was sit down in the middle of the chaos and sob out the day's frustrations, adding to the volume of liquid at my feet.

But in the midst of dyed purple towels and rags, murky-red mop water, stickiness everywhere, a beeping oven and a vibrating cell—I suddenly laughed aloud! I may not have anyone to help me clean up the mess, but I wasn't really alone. I may be sweating and juggling eight things at once, but I was going to have a relaxing evening with my friends over a huge, delicious dinner. It may smell like some kind of winery in my kitchen, but I felt profoundly grateful for all the good in my life.

At that I began to sing. My poor neighbor probably heard, but I didn't care. I sang those darn-early Christmas carols at the top of my lungs as I wiped up every last drop of that intolerable wine.

COURTNEY CONOVER

The Thanksgiving Dinner That Didn't

WHAT I DID: Accept Aunt June's invitation to Thanksgiving dinner.

Why: A momentary lapse of sanity that was invariably prompted by a need to make nice because, well, it was the holidays.

Requisite tools for the task: a) a cell phone, b) a landline, c) the ability to practice clairvoyance.

The rub: Even if you acquire said tools, you would still be facing an uphill battle because understanding Aunt June—and not to mention pleasing her—requires a level of skill and tenacity not unlike that which is seen in a James Bond film.

Here's what happened.

One Saturday in late October, I was enjoying coffee with my mother in her dining room.

"Aunt June wants to have Thanksgiving at her place," my mother mentioned casually. "Again."

Oh, yeah. Aunt June had hosted dinner last year. I had forgotten. Come to think of it, I hadn't given much thought to the coordination of

---

Courtney Conover is a wife, writer, and yoga enthusiast who is unsuccessfully trying to wean herself off eBay. When she's not writing or doing upward dog, she's on the never-ending quest to become more organized. She recently completed her first novel. Visit her online at www.courtneyconover.com.

this year's feast, either. Though my husband, Scott, and I were thankful to live in a home that begged to be entertained in, my husband's career as a chef often put the proverbial kibosh on hosting many holiday gatherings. (Culinary arts is virtually a 24-hour industry.) My husband didn't yet know if he would have to work on Thanksgiving, and I couldn't imagine inviting family over in his absence. (Not to mention that I can't cook; the thought of learning under the tutelage of a professional—even if he is my husband—gives me performance anxiety.)

Besides, I was looking forward to my mother hosting dinner this year. She had yet to christen her new condo with a large, festive meal. (The Chinese take-out smorgasbord we had indulged in last month didn't count.) I knew my mom wanted to host Thanksgiving, too. Furthermore, my mom had been reminding me all year that she never cooked her turkey from last Thanksgiving, and it had to be cooked this year so as not to go to waste. The turkey was burning a hole in her freezer.

"Yes," I replied. "I'll go to Aunt June's. And Scott, too. If he doesn't have to work."

Flash forward to a week before Thanksgiving. My mother and I hadn't heard a word from Aunt June. We all live relatively close to each other, but life generally gets in the way of regular telephone chats. A pathetic excuse for apathy, I know, but I'm only telling the truth. I knew that calling other relatives on my mom's side to get the who's-bringing-what run-down would prove futile, as they tend to do their own thing with their immediate families and prospective in-laws on Thanksgiving.

If we wanted to know what was happening, we would have to call Aunt June, for she alone held the skeleton key to this year's itinerary.

If you detect that I was hemming and hawing over calling Aunt June, you're spot on. It's not that I don't like Aunt June, it's... well, I'll just say it: She frightens me. In order for you to adequately understand my hesitation, allow me to enlighten you on the complexity that is Aunt June. Not to be a basket of clichés here, but Aunt June is tough as nails—with an acid tongue to boot. When she was a child, her own father had nicknamed her "fish woman," prompted by the obvious parallels between her acrimonious personality and that of a fisherman's wife.

In the spirit of procrastination, I put off calling her.

Then came the call from my mother, which, looking back, I should have considered a cosmic hint of things to come. She had called Aunt June, who had been mysteriously vague about Thanksgiving Day plans.

"I still don't know what I'm bringing... and I still don't know what time dinner is," my mom said with a hint of dismay.

"Did you tell her you already have a turkey?" I was secretly hoping that my mother had conveniently omitted that it had been lying in her freezer for the better part of a year. (Yes, culinary conjecture contends that the bird was safe to eat, but Lord only knows what Aunt June would have to say about that.)

"She doesn't want turkey. She said she's making a roast or something," my mom said dismissively.

No turkey? On Thanksgiving? I'm an equal opportunity carnivore, but choosing red meat over turkey on Thanksgiving is downright sacrilegious.

This was officially strike one.

"So you're still making a Snicker's cake, right?"

My mother's Snicker's cake. Named for the candy bar, my mother had pilfered the chocolate-caramel-peanut recipe from some cookbook back in the 1980s. It has since become her signature. I regarded the Snicker's cake as the eighth food group.

"Nope. She said her pecan pie will serve as dessert."

I felt my jaw clench. Strike two.

"So," my mother continued, "I offered to make the macaroni and cheese..." her voice trailed off.

"And?"

"She said it didn't quite go with the menu."

Strike three.

"So all we've got is some red meat, a pecan pie, and no start time," I recapped.

"Yup."

By 9 P.M. on Monday—a mere three days before Thanksgiving—I couldn't put it off any longer. I hadn't heard from Aunt June so I had to call her. Plus, Scott, who thankfully had Thanksgiving off, was asking me what dish we were supposed to bring.

I picked up my cell phone, dialed, and began to pace in the hallway.

"Hello?"

My voice caught in my throat. "Hey, Auntie. It's Courtney," I sputtered, feigning cheerfulness. Virtually everyone has caller ID these days, but I still felt the need to identify myself.

"Grumpff."

What was that? A hello? An oh, you, again? I decided it was somewhere in the middle. Regardless, it wasn't exactly pleasant. I continued.

"So what time is dinner, and what do you want us to bring—"

"I don't know yet," she cut me off. "I'll have to call you back."

"Oh...all right," I acquiesced. Clearly, she didn't want to talk. I wanted to put us both out of our misery. "I'll talk to you later," I said, followed by an I'm-fine-you're-fine-everybody's-fine chuckle.

Click.

I looked down at my phone. What had just happened? I called my mother and regaled her with the debacle. She sighed harshly; I could picture her shaking her head.

"Well, I'm gonna start thawing the turkey," my mother said decidedly. "Come hell or high water, I'm cooking it this Thanksgiving."

I went about the next few days both consciously and unconsciously anticipating Aunt June's call. Suffice it to say, when my mother and I hadn't heard from her by Wednesday night, I was mildly depressed. How could this dinner possibly be enjoyable? I wondered. But I also kept alive a flicker of hope that maybe—just maybe—Aunt June had reneged and didn't want to host dinner after all. If we hadn't heard from her, what were we supposed to think? I know, I know, one could argue that you technically don't need an invitation to go to a family member's home. But the fact remained: If somebody tells me they'll call with a time for me to come over, my M.O. would not be to just come over unannounced if I never hear from them. Especially if the host is Aunt June. Hell, she's liable to open the door and throw a pie (or Snicker's cake) in your face.

After dinner I dozed off on the couch, and a horrifically real nightmare infiltrated my subconscious. I dreamt that Aunt June called, screaming and frantic, to inform me that dinner was to start in 30 minutes. It takes me about ten minutes to drive to her house, mind you, so that left only 20 minutes to go to the store, shop, and whip up something edible. Yeah, right. I can't even make a grilled cheese sandwich in 20 minutes. That was why this was a nightmare. I awoke sweaty, dazed, and semi-fearful that this "dream" might become a reality. But with each passing moment, logic told me that dinner wasn't going to be at Aunt June's. Miraculously, I fell back to sleep.

Early Thanksgiving morning, Scott and I were awakened by my bleating cell phone. After fumbling to unplug it from the charger, I looked at the display and—for a fleeting second—saw that it was Aunt June. And then the call went into voicemail. I looked at Scott worriedly.

"Well, you knew this was coming," he said with his head planted on his pillow.

I slid under the comforter and pulled it over my head.

Then the phone rang. This time, the landline. Seconds later, Aunt June's voice was filtering through the answering machine.

"Jeez," I spat. "I don't hear from her for weeks, and now, Thanksgiving morning, she's got Lo-Jack. What's she going to do next, knock on our bedroom window?" I stopped talking. Better not to tempt fate, I decided.

"You have to tell her," Scott said blankly.

Yes. I had to tell Aunt June that Scott and I were having Thanksgiving dinner. At my mom's.

"Well, we haven't heard from her!" I said defensively.

"It's not me you have to convince," Scott said.

So I called Aunt June. As her phone rang, I could feel my heart beating in my teeth.

"Hello?" she answered.

Of course, she sounded more cheerful today.

"Dinner's at 3:30 . . . does that work for you?" she continued.

This was going to end very, very badly. But there was no turning back now. The bell had rung, we were in the ring, and the gloves were this close to coming off.

"Hey, Auntie, um, we're going to my mom's for dinner . . . we hadn't heard from you so we figured you weren't—"

And that's when she blew. My words were the proverbial match to the powder keg.

"WHHAAAAT????" HOW COULD YOU ASSUME THAT?!!!"

What ensued for the next ten minutes was the verbal equivalent of a tsunami. I was feeling a lot of heat all of a sudden. Could it have been that Aunt June's ire was traveling through sound waves, bouncing off the nearest cellular tower, and emanating through my cell phone? My paranoia told me it was possible.

I tried to interject but was sent reeling into the corner of the ring after each attempt. "Aunt June, can I talk?"

"HOW INSENSITIVE!"

"Can I say something?"

"I COOKED A TON . . ." Her ranting continued like a steamroller.

"Okay. I'll just sit here and breathe. Just tell me when I'm allowed to talk so we can have a civilized conversation." I was quite proud of myself for the new backbone I had just grown.

Not to be outdone, Aunt June came right back. "Yes, you just sit there and breathe!"

Aunt June actually believed that she had told us not to bring anything to dinner, and she felt completely justified in not calling us until Thanksgiving morning about a dinner that was to take place six hours from now. She went on to say that if we were unsure, we should have called her. Never mind the fact that when a host decides to have a gathering, she should probably be able to tell guests the time. Particularly when the gathering is, oh, Thanksgiving—a holiday that is the same day every year. Is that too much to ask?

Why ask why. Now, I was the one shaking my head.

Scott and I had dinner at my mother's. She whipped up a traditional feast of savory favorites, including macaroni and cheese and her famous Snicker's cake. I don't know what Aunt June did, but since she probably had enough food to feed a small army, I figure she didn't go hungry.

If I've learned anything this Thanksgiving, it's this: when it comes to Aunt June and holiday meals, mind reading is as necessary an ingredient as salt and pepper.

And I learned this: a properly thawed, slowly cooked year-old frozen turkey can taste divine.

CAROL M. GREEN

Thanksgiving Phobia

MOST FOLKS have some kind of holiday phobia. Whether it is in connection with the holiday itself, or the expectations placed on the holiday, the phobias exist and they are as varied as the individuals who suffer from them. For instance, single people might prefer to avoid Valentine's Day altogether, while those from a large clan may simply be overwhelmed with the demands of gift-giving at Christmastime. The unbeliever might consider the Christian holiday a nuisance to be endured.

For me, that holiday is Thanksgiving. Oh, it's not the holiday's fault. I am generally a grateful person. It isn't the food's fault. I love turkey, pumpkin pie, and cranberries. I also love to cook. I hate to boast, but I make the best homemade turkey stuffing anyone I know has ever eaten! No, it's not the holiday's fault. I blame it on the mishaps.

Mishap Number One: I was exhausted on Thanksgiving Day. Having recently discovered I was expecting our second child, I couldn't bring myself to assist the other womenfolk in clean-up of the Thanksgiving meal. Two days later, I was no longer expecting.

As a child, Carol Green entertained herself with make-believe friends and imagined places. She believes that people lead remarkable lives; their stories just fail to be told. She strives to illustrate this point through her essays and fiction. You can read more in her book, Gold Pans and Iron Skillets.

Doctors call it an "Oops"—a baby that wasn't really a baby, so the mother's body decides to get rid of it.

Mishap Number Two: The following year, we were the proud parents of a newborn boy who spent five days in the hospital suffering from pneumonia.

Mishap Number Three: The next year, we were living with my in-laws awaiting purchase of a new home. The loan almost did not go through! Great stress!

Additional Mishaps: Very few stores are open on Thanksgiving Day. Oh, the grocery stores stay open for last-minute emergency items like celery and whipping cream, but plumbing supply stores are dark, cold, and locked up for the weekend. We discovered this when I clogged the kitchen drain with too many potato peels! Last year, my still-relatively-young husband had a heart that decided it was time to receive a pacemaker. Happy Thanksgiving to us!

Because I am aware of my Thanksgiving phobia, I approach the holiday with measured anticipation. I am determined to put few expectations on my Thanksgiving celebration. Whatever goes well is great. Whatever doesn't go well is par. I prepared in advance. Turkey thawed. Bread cubes dried. Pies baked. Last-minute shopping avoided. What could go wrong? I wasn't even hosting the meal. Therein lay the problem.

I have never had a turkey roasted in a bag fail to be done as expected. I even gave him extra time in the oven. We pulled him out of the oven, sliced him open and gasped! Thankfully, I had prepared extra stuffing in a crock pot. Did I mention how great my stuffing is? We shoved the turkey, bag and all, into a second bag, stuffed it all in the oven, and set the timer for additional cooking time. Then we traveled 20 miles east to dinner—no turkey in hand. After dinner, we traveled 20 miles west to salvage our bird. Having removed his flesh from the bones and stored it safely in the refrigerator, we then made another 48-mile trek east to eat a piece of pie and returned 48 miles west to sleep. Maybe next year we'll just stay home.

Here is the irony of it all. The well-done turkey was allowed to cool in the bag. It was undoubtedly the best turkey I have ever roasted! For that, I am thankful!

WILLIAM KENNY

My Dear Uncle Harold

EVERY YEAR as Thanksgiving approached, I always found myself wistfully thinking of my dear Uncle Harold. He was the centerpiece of every family Thanksgiving celebration for more than 25 years. There was one simple reason for this great family legacy. Uncle Harold had the ability to render an entire group of heathens quiet and reverent for two plus minutes by virtue of being the only family member that could pray and sound like he meant it. He wasn't just good; he was magnificent and his prayers were Orwellian in scope. Sometimes they went on for more than the allotted two minutes and the gravy got cold. And then there was the year, 1981, I think it was, where he simply wouldn't stop and mold formed on the mashed potatoes. Of course, we didn't dare complain because it was during those times that Uncle Harold was really in spirit and you really didn't want to mess with spirit, at least not anything you couldn't drink, if you belonged to our family. The only thing we ever had to worry about was the food, the homemade schnapps, and having enough dinner trays because "Grace" was Uncle Harold's domain, and he wasn't about to give it up. He was so good, in fact, it was as if Moses himself had stopped by to give a helping hand. Every

---

William Kenny is sixty years of age and spent thirty years in the restaurant industry. For the last three years, he has been writing, working on his photography skills and marketing on the Internet. He currently lives in beautiful Denver, Colorado, and is an avid hiker and photographer.

Thanksgiving, Uncle Harold literally kicked "Grace" through the family goalposts (The Lions and Packers being respectfully turned off), and thus, properly blessed, we could get on with the eating and drinking—the drinking always carrying the day.

Where Michael Jordan was the face of the NBA, my Uncle Harold was the face of "Grace" throughout my entire adult life. In the early years while living far away from home, I sometimes had to travel more than a thousand miles to get back for the Thanksgiving holiday. But with the thought of Uncle Harold giving grace, those two magical minutes or longer, and wondering whether you might even be featured ("Lord, bless Bill and be with him on his long journey home to Utah"), it always sustained me as the freeway sign pointed out Des Moines was still 578 miles away. Being featured in Uncle Harold's Thanksgiving prayer actually created another smaller but lucrative family tradition, the wager. There were always three or four side bets as to who was going to be featured in that year's prayer. I was always blessed with a better than 50 percent chance because of the sacrifice of distance traveled, and besides, I hadn't been around to piss Uncle Harold off. I usually wagered ten bucks on myself and more often than not I collected some sizable gas money from relatives struggling with major drinking problems.

Where Uncle Harold acquired this unique ability is somewhat of a mystery to me. He owned a small corn roller mill company in Cedar Falls, Iowa, and was married to my Dad's sister Mae. I guess if you own a corn roller mill company in Iowa you were definitely Somebody! They were church-going folks and he held church-going titles like "Elder" and "Deacon" and such. Their three kids grew up to be fine young adults with the youngest son, John, becoming a missionary in South America. Despite all this, Uncle Harold also had a dark side.

He just might have been the meanest, most demanding customer to ever step foot in a restaurant. I was especially sensitive to this as I was a big shot in the restaurant industry at the time. I remember being stunned one day as I watched the Michael Jordan of "Grace" reduce a poor waitress into a stuttering, tearful heap. I sometimes felt like maybe he was a reincarnated former slave owner from the early 1800s. I could visualize him giving the lead slave Tobias a few last instructions just before gathering the family in the wagon and riding off to Sunday morning church.

Of course, there was also the fact that Uncle Harold was an alcoholic, and maybe his ability to send back the pork fritters for a third time and give the perfect prayer came from channeling spirit through the drinking of it. There was also the time I watched Uncle Harold jump off the roof of his house while drunk, thus breaking his leg. There he was, the church-going elder, screaming "Geronimo!" and hurtling through the air, arms flailing, glasses askew, right into his neighbor's juniper bush. Somehow for me that just didn't fit the profile of a man who could take a group of heathens and turn them into pious, grateful, God-fearing folk at Thanksgiving time. The family decided to keep that little episode under wraps. No sense tarnishing the man's hard-earned reputation. Every year, when it came down to crunch time, Uncle Harold held every member of the family in the palm of his hand. That was all that mattered.

Generally, my mother would give the call for dinner. It sounded something like this: "Hey everybody! It's time to eat dinner! Uncle Harold, would you please say grace?" The last part was totally unnecessary because even my three-year-old niece Emily knew who the King of Grace was. So with everyone putting down their glasses of beer, schnapps, Gallo Chardonnay, shots of Jimmy Beam, and with my youngest brother Steve outside puking in a ditch next to the driveway, Uncle Harold, hands clasped reverently in front of him, would sidle up to the table with head bowed. Of course, at that very moment, my cousin's husband, Larry, would be in the middle of slurring another dirty joke.

Fortunately for us, Uncle Harold always started grace off with the famous "Clearing of the throat call," which was sort of like the bugler at the Kentucky Derby, and this silenced everybody and everything. Even the cows and chickens outside stood quietly when they heard the clearing of the throat. Outside, my brother Steve would slowly roll over onto his side and wipe his face off out of respect, and Larry would stop mid-punch line and lower his head. Like a great tenor, my uncle would stand stoically, moving nary a muscle. There'd be one more clearing of the throat, "Aahhrruummpphh, aahhhrrruuummmpphh." "For God's sake, I'd think to myself, put it in gear will ya?"

Then he'd begin: "Dear Heavenly Father, we ask that you bless this glorious food before us this day." I always liked that first sentence. When you're hungry, there's nothing better than blessed mashed potatoes, turkey and those little green snow peas. I would start to drool. "And Lord, bless each and every one of our assembled family here today. Bless their families and be with my nephew, Bill, on his long and arduous journey back to Utah."

SCORE! Boy did I like getting top billing in Uncle Harold's prayers! While he continued, I totaled up my take. Out of the corner of my eye, I saw my brother-in-law shaking his head in disgust and mouthing the word "Damn!" Harold continued, "Lord, we ask that you bless those that are away from their families on this day, and we ask that you be with those that have lost loved ones this past year." God, what style he had. "Be with each of us on this most special day, and help us remember the many blessings that thou hast bestowed upon us, LEST WE FORGET!" That part of grace was the result of him having to listen to a family member or two bitching about the President and his handling of political affairs—a man Uncle Harold had voted for. It was tough being a Republican in a Socialist state like Iowa. "Lord, we also ask you to bless the marriage of Carla and Gilbert."

Huh? Carla and Gilbert! Who in the hell were Carla and Gilbert? I did a quick mental review of the family tree and there wasn't a Carla or Gilbert to be found. I snuck a quick peek and didn't see anybody that could be mistaken for Carla or Gilbert. There were plenty of wide-eyed looks my way wondering if maybe I knew who the mysterious Carla and Gilbert were. Oh, well, even the great ones slip up once in awhile.

He continued, "We bless and rejoice in the knowing that you sent your son, Jesus, here so that we may be saved." At this point, it was so quiet you could hear a pin drop. Nobody, I mean nobody, wanted to be caught glancing around, fidgeting, snickering, or passing gas at this juncture lest they be struck down by a bolt of lightning with Uncle Harold shouting, "Smite the heathen and send him to everlasting hell!" Then there would be the dramatic five-second pause before

Uncle Harold said, "We ask these blessings in thy name, Amen." There would be a moment of silence as everybody absorbed the moment. Then raising their heads they'd smile, thank Uncle Harold, and become heathens once again until the following Thanksgiving. With a volunteer heading out to fetch my brother Steve, the scrum to eat would begin.

Though hungry, I was always just a little sad and depressed at this point because Uncle Harold went back to being the real Uncle Harold, and that quiet couple of minutes had now become a scene of utter chaos as the heathens fought over drumsticks, macadamia nut casserole and celery sticks. Someone inevitably always got sliced up a bit in the jostling for the best pieces of turkey, so you really had to have your head on a swivel right after grace. I sadly realized that someday, the two minutes or more with Uncle Harold would be but a fond memory, and I hoped and prayed I had at least a couple more years of seeing him, head bowed, standing reverently in front of the turkey and mashed potatoes. All in all, it was always good to be home with my family even if they were heathens. The food and drink was truly a blessing, and thankfully, my brother Steve had stopped puking and was now quietly sleeping it off in the basement. Another wonderful Thanksgiving Day was underway and, if you were unfortunately related to these people, you might as well suck it up and enjoy yourself. Besides, I knew I had once again witnessed the master at work and I was most grateful.

Late in the day, we would carry Uncle Harold out to his car, a victim of the schnapps. We always knew he was in good hands because Aunt Mae insisted on driving home and she was into abstinence, especially since the day he'd barreled through Clyde Witworth's corn crib while missing the main turnoff to Highway 20. Sadly, the fateful day did toll and Uncle Harold passed away. The following year, my cousin's husband Larry said grace, but he slurred his words so much, we were left totally befuddled. Then the next year, my "born again" brother, Gary, said grace and actually got booed mid-prayer, which worried me to no end. Was it possible for your food to be blessed if the guests were booing the Grace Giver? Gary was way too conversational in style when praying, and the sudden confessing of his sins made the rest of us a tad queasy. Saying grace to a family trained over the years in a style only Uncle Harold could produce meant amateurs weren't welcome.

We eventually decided to scratch grace from the program, what with Uncle Harold being gone and knowing that we were all a bunch of heathens anyway. There was no sense muddying up a proud family tradition, and besides, we didn't want to know the latest dirt on Gary. So now each year, I'm left to my memories of Uncle Harold. Why, when I quietly close my eyes just before dinner, I can still hear him clearing his throat. Amen to that!

VINCENT J. TOMEO

November 23, 1983

I never liked my brother
until one day he came to visit our mother
He wanted to see her one last time
before he died

Weeks before he had ordered a custom made suit with pads
and he wore a wig of light brown wavy hair parted on the right

Thanksgiving Day
I hid mama's glasses so she could not see

Mama searched all over the house for her glasses
I am always losing my glasses she said
why didn't I have a second pair made? Where are my glasses?
did you see my glasses? No, mama

I felt terrible
I had locked mama's glasses in my car's glove compartment
knowing mama would never look there
Robert sat across the table he was unable to eat
Christine distracted mama and put some of his turkey on my plate

At the end of the evening he hugged mama
and mama hugged him back and straightened his hair

After he left mama said he looked tired but well
she liked his new suit although she did not like his new hair style

Vincent J. Tomeo has been published in The New York Times, Comstock Review, Mid-America Poetry Review, EDGZ, Spires, Tiger's Eye, ByLine, Mudfish, The Blind Man's Rainbow, The NeoVictorian/Cochlea, The Latin Staff Review, *and* Grandmother Earth (VII through XI), *and has published 593 poems to date.*

PAULA TIMPSON

Fry Dough & Sitting With Grandpa

EVERY THANKSGIVING, I'd sit alone, with my grandpa, in grandma's kitchen, the scent of heavenly Italian foods and Turkey with trimmings... all around... I liked to be with him in the peace of a big holiday celebration; just us two quietly eating; listening to the laughter and talk coming from the living room and dining room... We'd always take our time and be the last ones to finish up our meal. Grandpa would always ask me if I like mince pie and I'd always say no... I wanted grandma's fry dough more than anything! Watching her at the stove, in her white apron, with a big smile on her face as she created wonderful love in food for her family... No place I'd rather be at that moment! Thanksgiving, to my heart, has always been the true thanks and simple joys of feeling my family all together, needing nothing but the pure love we always received from heaven and on earth! Grandma's green eyes alight with so much Love... Love, Paula

Paula Timpson breathes poetry daily, and has a "spirit series" of poetry books and a poetry ministry! http://paulaspoetryworld.blogspot.com

ERIKA HOFFMAN

Curse the Turkey—Pass the Pepto

MEMORIES OF THANKSGIVINGS PAST rank up there with childhood tooth fillings minus anesthesia. I can't recall a single one from my childhood in the 50s, youth in the 60s, or college years, the 70s, that wasn't marred.

When we were youngsters, Grandma Spike fixed the meal. (Dad nicknamed her "Spike" because she was fat; I never learned her given name till age 11 when I got scolded by my aunt for my impudence. "But that's her name," I insisted.) On Turkey Day, cousins burst in and out of her home, aunt and uncle hovered, and one weird kin, Cousin Louis, appeared. Louis—a bookkeeper, never married, and Dad's second cousin twice removed, "but not far enough," my brother added—was odd.

Louey lived with his mother until she passed. Then it fell to Grandma Spike to include him in holiday repasts.

Louey clicked or clucked his tongue, had facial ticks, and spoke at a strange tempo; his laugh was forced, nasal, and nerdy. Mom thought him a genius because he'd rattle off dates of all the

---

Erika Hoffman is a wife, mother, daughter/caregiver, former teacher, and author of more than 48 published articles and one novel. Her novel, published by Comfort Publishing, is called Secrets, Lies, and Grace. *Her e-mail address is: bhoffman@nc.rr.com.*

birthdays, anniversaries, and deaths in everyone's family. "What a memory you have, Louey!" my mother flattered. I thought this super power just one more peculiarity in a wide range of eccentricities. He slurped his food and scraped the tines of his fork on the china. "Do you know Louey was present at your grandparents' wedding?" Mom marveled. When we returned home after the feast, violently ill, Mom reasoned we'd picked up a bug. I suspected weird Louey as the carrier.

With my grandparents' passing, the Thanksgiving celebration fell to Mom; she included Louey. "Who else will invite him?" she explained. No argument there. He never said much to my sister or me, but his eyes sparkled blue when my brother entered the room. He'd pat the couch, wanting my brother to sit close by him as we waited for the meal to commence.

Mom prepared shrimp or herring as an appetizer, but Louey was allergic to seafood. So Mom served him his own fruit cocktail. He had definite views on what he'd eat or not eat. In high school, I read Melville's story, "Bartleby the Scrivener," about the social misfit who always answered, "I'd prefer not," to any and all requests. Louey was Bartleby incarnate.

Each Thanksgiving, I was as certain of contracting a case of cramps, nausea, and vomiting as I was of what Louey would give us for Christmas—a book. Louey stared at his shoes as he thrust the present toward me. "I've never read *Heidi* before. Thanks, Cousin Louey!"

By 18, I had named the malady, "Lethal Louey's Thanksgiving gift." He carried some super bug that only afflicted normal folks like me. I loathed this holiday and kissed the air as the French do rather than have any tactile contact with Cousin Contagious.

My sophomore year in college, I asked Mom, "Do we have to include Louey?"

"Yes."

"I don't want to spend vacation genuflecting over the commode."

"Ridiculous! Maybe you're not using common sense or good hygiene. Do you wear rubbers over your shoes in the rain?"

"Geez!"

"Your dad sits next to him every year and never catches so much as a sneeze!"

"They have the same genetic make-up—some weird, mutant German gene!"

"We can be gracious at Thanksgiving! Louey has never been lucky enough to have a family! Case closed!"

"Luck? Did you ever notice that huge wart taking over his chin?"

So the Terminator/Contaminator—also known as unlucky Louey—kept coming every year. As he aged, he became stranger. One year, he called Mom at the last minute to announce he'd booked a flight to Arizona to grace Dad's sister with his presence. He'd decided the Northeast winters were injurious to his health.

"Hallelujah! For once, we won't break bread with Typhoid Mary—I mean, Lethal Louey," I declared. "But the downside is I won't get the gift of last century's bestseller! Shucks."

"You're mean," said Mom.

"Gosh, we won't get to hear him conjugate Latin verbs he learned 50 years ago!" So secure of my diagnostic abilities of our Thanksgiving disease, I planned an evening out—a thought hitherto verboten. That Thanksgiving, I engaged in conspicuous consumption with seconds and thirds of the stuffing! My prayers answered, I enjoyed feasting free of phobia and Imodium A-D.

That night found me stooped in the downward-dog position. Likewise bent were Mom, sister, and brother. Only Dad escaped the turkey's revenge.

Still looking like faded-out dishrags a day later, we congregated over bland rice and hot tea, discussing our recent near-death experience. Mom speculated on the origin of our shared stomach virus. The television droned on in the den. I listened with one ear to Mom's admonitions: "Keep your head dry when it rains. Put some Vick's vapor rub right beneath your nose to catch germs." In the background, I heard a news report warning folks about sticking their stuffing inside the bird. Bacteria grows in its cavity, the reporter explained, and if the moist stuffing isn't thoroughly cooked, food poisoning will result.

"All these years, you kids have blamed poor, old, lonesome Louey—oddball that he is—for various sicknesses. Why, this year proves it wasn't him since he was not even…"

"You're right!" I exclaimed, pushing back my chair as I leaped up. Heads swiveled towards me. "It's not Lethal Louey; it's ptomaine Turkey!"

"What?" said my sister.

"Mom leaves that butterball out all night on the counter and then spoons the dressing in the next morning. She hates a dry turkey. Germs grow 'cause the bird's perched out of the fridge, and they all get soaked up in the dressing."

"Dad never eats stuffing," my sister remarked.

"Voila! Mystery solved," I said and sat down. "Case closed."

"Louey's not the culprit?" said my sister.

"That's how my mom cooked it and your dad's mom and…" said my mother.

"When you were a kid, did you get belly aches on Thanksgiving?" I asked.

"I never could remember to wear a slicker in the rain." Mom smiled.

"So my cousin twice removed has been exonerated?" asked Dad.

"Still he gives me the heebie jeebies," I said.

"You? He pats my knee," announced my brother.

"Maybe he'll like the oven-dry climate and relocate out there in the desert?" Mom suggested.

"Aunt Trudy has sons," quipped my brother.

"Dream on," I said. You think a guy who won't let food groups touch on a plate, who calls mayonnaise 'women's food,' and who claims a casserole is a week's worth of leftovers dumped together—a guy like that is going to eat an enchilada with mole sauce and refried beans?"

"Feeding Louey is our little stab at doing the right thing on Thanskgiving, like folks spending the day serving the homeless," reasoned Mom.

"Think what we'd miss if he didn't come. All those death dates of scores of Bavarians! Why watch a football game, like the rest of America, when we are blessed with live entertainment like Louey?" I proclaimed.

"No stuffing next year," announced Mom. "I'll serve red cabbage, pickled beets, and rhubarb pie. Louey told me those were his favorites."

My stomach gurgled. I checked the clock to see how much longer before I'd sup on safe, FDA-approved, dried-out airplane cuisine. Tastiness is overrated.

ANNA JONES

Dawn

WE WRAP OUR NECKS with woolen scarves and button up our coats to simply trudge from the car to the old, weather-beaten farmhouse. It's Thanksgiving Day, and as the wind whips from the flat farmland, I think about how much colder it always is at my grandpa's house in Kentucky. My dad's whole side of the family gathers for these 24 hours to consume massive amounts of turkey, pumpkin pie, and green bean casserole. Well, I'm not supposed to eat the green bean casserole—and neither is my brother, mom, or dad. Each year, on the car ride down, somewhere in between switching out *The Music Man* to the Doobie Brothers, my dad gives us strict orders: "Remember—Aunt Maureen always makes green bean casserole. Do *not* eat the green bean casserole."

If you could see my Aunt Maureen's kitchen, you would know why these orders are imperative. The moment you walk inside, the pungent smell of year-old kitty litter swirls around your nostrils. Several cats have made a home out of the kitchen counter, and honestly, I'm not sure if there is a bottle of Clorox in the entire household.

We're reminded of the urgency of avoiding the contaminated dish as the whole family gathers in the dining room to bless the food. Just as we are all about to close our eyes and bow our heads, I glance at

---

Anna Jones resides in Huntington, West Virginia, where she writes and studies non-fiction and poetry. She tutors undergraduate students in composition at the Marshall University Writing Center.

my dad. He locks his eyes with mine, points conspicuously to the casserole, and makes a sharp cutting motion across his neck.

We eat, and I remember why we only spend these 24 hours together each year. I think we need the whole year to forget. My mom, magically, becomes more conservative than she is the remaining 364 days of the year, and Aunt Maureen, in response, exchanges cutting political remarks with her. This is our dinnertime conversation, and once we are all too full to stand ourselves anymore, we disperse into separate corners of the farmhouse.

Aunt Maureen and I find ourselves alone together in the living room, and she pulls out an aged family photo album. I make small talk—"Wow! I'm so full. Oh yes, of course I loved your casserole"—as she narrates picture after picture.

"This is when your father and I went sledding during the blizzard of '72," she says after showing me a black-and-white photo of a New York snowstorm. She flips the page and there is a beachside picture of my dad, hardly an adult, with his arm around some busty brunette.

"That's Dawn," my aunt said to me with suspiciously cutting eyes. "Do you know Dawn?"

She doesn't wait for my response—"Oh you know, she was just *beautiful*, vivacious, outgoing, just perfect, really. Perfect for your dad."

I see her glance toward the window. Outside, my dad and my brother are tossing a football. I hear her murmur under her breath, "*The type of woman we thought he would marry . . .*"

I can see my mom in the dining room. She is alone, gathering up our used napkins, spraying and wiping down the table.

On the car ride home, my mom repeats my aunt's (clearly heinous) political views. My dad talks about the cold weather, the juiciness of this year's turkey, and the needed repairs of the farmhouse. I admit to eating the green bean casserole.

CHARLES WEST

A Thanksgiving Anecdote

MONDAY MORNING. First period. The end of first period and I've forgotten to take roll. I get all the W's before an unexcused absence rears its ugly head. "Mr. Willis, do you have an absence slip?"

"I haven't been absent."

"You were absent all last week." The bell rang and Mr. Willis' classmates cleared the classroom much quicker than they drifted in. Mr. Willis paused at my desk.

"I didn't hear you," he said. "The bell rang."

"You need an absence slip for last week."

Young Mr. Willis laughed. In all my years of asking for an absence slip, his reaction was unusual. It may actually have been a first had it not been for Patrick Green several years ago, whose response to every question was laughter. Mr. Green disappeared from the attendance rolls immediately following the undercover drug bust of 2003.

"And what is so humorous?" I asked, adding my disappointed teacher face.

Charles West is a teacher and writer living and working in central California. He has published poetry, fiction and non-fiction in a variety of publications. His novel, A Sacred Disc, *was published in 2000 by Salvo Press.*

"You crack me up, Mr. West." He laughed again. "It was vacation," he said.

"What vacation?" I asked, replacing the disappointed teacher face with the confused teacher face.

"Thanksgiving," he said, still smiling. "Last week was Thanksgiving. We do get the whole week off, don't we?"

"That's right," I said. "However, there's just one small problem there, Mr. Willis." There was a pause while I waited for Mr. Willis to identify the problem. When he failed to do so, I gave him the answer: "Mr. Willis, we are currently in the month of October. Thanksgiving is in November."

"No, it was last Thursday," he insisted. "I swear."

"Mr. Willis, last Thursday was definitely not Thanksgiving. Were government offices closed? No. Were the Dallas Cowboys playing? No. Were the Detroit Lions playing? No. Did you see the Macy's Day Parade? No. Did you catch a TV news report on how busy holiday travel is? No. Was Save Mart giving away a free turkey with every $100 purchase? No. On Friday was there an early morning rush on large retail establishments, known as Black Friday? No. That's because all these things occur on Thanksgiving, which is on the fourth Thursday of November. We are currently in the month of October, a month more commonly associated with Halloween, which also hasn't happened yet."

I suddenly noticed that I now had a roomful of glassy-eyed juniors, no doubt waiting for some sort of transfer of knowledge. The bell rang. "Mr. Willis, we will have to continue this another time. Go to your second period."

I went through the rest of the day slightly annoyed by my interaction with young Mr. Willis. I was in the process of loading my tote bag with a stack of unmarked quizzes when Mr. Willis reappeared. He handed me a calendar and said, "See?"

"See what?"

"October 11."

"What about it?"

"Look at it."

I looked at it. "Columbus Day?"

"Underneath."

I looked at the calendar. Underneath Columbus Day was the word, "Thanksgiving," followed by the letter *C* in parentheses.

"The *C* stands for Canada. Last week was Canadian Thanksgiving."

"Oh, they have one, too?"

"Yes, in October."

"So . . . I get another one next month?"

"Yes, you do."

"Do I still need an absence slip?"

"No," I said, "I'll take care of it."

"See you tomorrow," he said, and left.

When I was the age of young Mr. Willis, Thanksgiving was the supreme holiday. A four-day weekend. No presents, no church, no Hallmark cards, a minimum of decorations. Just family and friends together for a single meal. That's how my family and friends say they feel, although I suspect there are actually some who prefer the free candy of Halloween and the presents of Christmas. As I locked my classroom door, I thought about how I would tell my friends about the dumb kid who stayed home the week of Canadian Thanksgiving. By the time I reached my car, however, I was reconsidering.

What could I tell them about young Mr. Willis, whose Thanksgiving seemed to be no different than a day in October. I would just have to repeat the same old Thanksgiving anecdotes. And I was looking forward to it.

PATRICK WILLIAMS

Soup Attempt for the Soul

IT HAS BEEN FIVE YEARS now since I said goodbye to my mother, sister, and stepfather. I walked directly out the front door as the yelling and screaming faded from a piercing volume to eventual silence. Each Thanksgiving since that significant day has demanded a fresh new way to occupy my time—without the standard Hallmark portrayal of one's large family gathered around an endless, full table, a glistening turkey in the center, and a father figure standing at the helm holding carving utensils. The first few years, I gathered with friends and their corresponding families; another year was even spent enjoying the bright lights of Atlantic City with a fellow coworker. This year, however, it will be spent alone and at home.

Most people cannot help but link the celebration of the seasons with great abundances of delicious food. Over time, I have accepted the fact that I lack even the simplest culinary expertise beyond boiling pasta or ordering Kung Pao Chicken. Still, this particular holiday break provides the time and opportunity to attempt tasks one

---

Patrick Williams, a full-time Civil Engineer, has enjoyed his occupation for many years. He has always remained truly passionate for entertaining those closest to him, mostly through exaggerated re-caps of everyday encounters. He lives in Philadelphia, Pennsylvania, with his two feline companions. This is his first essay.

might not normally perform. Therefore, I excitedly decided to cook a Thanksgiving meal for one person.

At this point, I would love to humorously describe how a miniature fire had set half of my kitchen ablaze. It would be funny, although predictable, to explain that my turkey had been burnt to a charred crisp after spending too much time in the oven. One might be amused if I had accidentally locked myself out of my house; resulting in an oddly fulfilling meal with an on-call locksmith. Despite what even I may have expected, the food that I had prepared was extremely edible and none of these entertaining scenarios played out that day.

It was only after my meal was finished, after shaving off the remaining turkey for a series of highly anticipated leftover sandwiches, that I had noticed the bare carcass. With the assistance of the Internet, I found that the frugal utilization of all purchased resources would be to make a turkey-based soup. Using a random recipe, I placed the remnants into a pot, set the contents to an initial boil, and relaxed in perpetual pride as I found myself playing the part of a truly domesticated bachelor.

I followed the directions and added my ingredients. After two hours, I opened the pot to stir. An array of my favorite seasonings and vegetables now simmered on the stove as the aroma filled the air. I had set my cell phone alarm for the proper cook time and continued to unwind on the couch, flipping the channels between football and sitcom reruns. After a grand total of four hours, the alarm clock sounded. I had set up a large bowl and searched for a proper ladle from the kitchen drawers to no avail. And then I removed the lid.

As I stood there, staring into the liquidless container, many different thoughts streamed through my mind. The obvious first reflection was that within the last two hours, I must have simply evaporated any progress I had made in the first two, leaving only bones and miscellaneous turkey meat simmering at the bottom of the pot. Crying would have been an over-the-top reaction to the unsuccessful experiment, as would even the slightest hint of disappointment or frustration. It was my life. It was not that there was symbolization of emptiness or failure that directly coincided with the feelings I have in my day-to-day life. Rather, it was that there is solace in the idea that if, against all logic and probability, there is a higher power than our own existence, he, she, or it could not help but be entertained by such a comedic notion. I have no diseases, nor am I burdened by the need of a wheelchair. I am just a lonely guy who can't make soup; and life could be a lot worse.

BETH LYNN CLEGG

Blurred Vision

MY IMAGINATION kicked into overdrive while heading out of Houston toward the piney woods of deep East Texas. I'd been invited to spend Thanksgiving with my daughter and son-in-law at his mother's home, along with other family members. Stories passed down from one generation to the next of ancestors sharing nature's bounty with Indians in the 1600s conjured up visions worthy of Currier and Ives depictions.

Eighteen miles east of Nacogdoches, my Ford Explorer dropped onto a red dirt road that wound its way under a dense canopy of pines, sweet gum, and oak for several enchanting miles before arriving at her home. For this city gal, who grew up in Austin, a visit with Jo was like entering a foreign land. In her late 70s, she still planted a large garden, mended fences, tended flower beds, preserved jams and jellies from various fruit trees, and fished for crappie from her pond.

With relatives arriving from distant cities, sleeping arrangements had been made in advance at several homes. My pillows and quilts would help provide restful sleep on a sofa in the living room or den of her three-bedroom, one-bath home. Although surprised to find numerous parked cars, I assumed the visitors would be moving on.

Beth Lynn Clegg, from Houston, Texas, has been published in a variety of genres since beginning her writing career after retiring from other endeavors. She enjoys church activities, gardening and reading when not involved with family and friends. She's a member of the Writers' League of Texas.

In my dreams! As sunlight gave way to dusk, then dark, those cars hadn't budged, nor had their occupants. It became clear that I was the one who'd be moving on. As in, moving on to sleep in my car. A flurry of obligatory protests were offered and rejected before I explained the obvious. As the only single adult, nothing else made sense.

After folding the back seats down, my nest took shape. Despite the cold, many trudged out to inspect my handiwork. It was suggested that mine was the best deal. No one would pull off covers or snore in my ear. I encouraged them to save their hot air to keep the house warm and sent them packing.

Then reality set in. Being locked in wasn't as reassuring as I'd thought, but there was no turning back now. The absence of city lights that had made previous visits so appealing now made my surroundings too dark on this moonless night. It was also way too quiet. Stop it! I shifted my mental dialogue. Should I sleep in my clothes? Pajamas are so much more comfortable. But what if someone knocks on the window, or I have to get out? Clothes won.

Once that battle abated, my attempt to find a comfortable position began. Who knew hips, ribs, and shoulder blades could create such conflict with a Detroit creation buffered by a too-thin layer of padding? I finally drifted off to sleep and wished I'd remained in dreamland. That wasn't to be. Nature called and there was the great-big-dark-as-pitch outdoors awaiting me.

My heart pounded in my ears when the overhead light made me an easy target for anyone waiting to grab me. Of course it was ridiculous, but knowing my thinking was illogical didn't help. Despite my irrational fears, the only thing attempting to grab me was a wind-chill sucking the air out of my lungs and freezing my posterior.

Recounting my nocturnal adventure led to riotous laughter, but there were no takers to trade accommodations. That's when I decided I would've been the best settler in the bunch. Here I was, the city slicker, second eldest, yet these young whippersnappers weren't up to the challenge of sleeping in my SUV.

While my memories are priceless, I must admit that Thanksgiving holiday of family feasting and fellowship wasn't quite the Currier and Ives moment I'd envisioned.

ANGIE REEDY

A Rock Castle Thanksgiving

HIGH ON A MISSOURI CLIFF stands a rock castle. Its windows look majestically over the river below and the cows grazing on the other side. A fire pit outside will soon be circled with folding chairs carried from Kansas, Illinois, Nebraska, and even Ohio. The abandoned observation area waits for guests to admire the beauty laid out below. And the wooden porch swing sways next to the leaf-covered stone throne room, where couples will sneak away to soak in time alone. This is our Thanksgiving home.

While many Americans chase their turkey and pumpkin pie with Black Friday ads and plans to hit the sales the next day, we finish our Thanksgiving feast with discussions of whether the next item on our agenda should be reading around the campfire, hiking to the river, or playing another round of the favorite board game of the year.

Before I even met her, and she was just the mother of this great guy I was dating, Carolyn reserved a cabin at a state park as a way to celebrate Thanksgiving and meet this new girl her son was dating. When Walter suggested I join his family for the holiday in a secluded

---

Angie Reedy is a freelance writer who lives in central Illinois with her husband and two children. She delights in finding evidences of God's extraordinary greatness in the ordinary happenings of life and blogs about them at www.realreedy.blogspot.com.

cabin, I jumped at the opportunity to spend eight hours in the car with him and a whole weekend with him in the woods.

We pulled up to that first little cabin, and arms soon embraced us in warmth I needed to feel. My parents had recently moved to the other side of the globe. My holidays needed tradition and they needed love. Even though I didn't officially belong to their family (yet), I received the prime bedroom and an immediate spot in the middle of family activities.

Isolated in the leaf-covered woods, we began a tradition that I wouldn't trade for anything.

Forced to move on from that original rustic cabin when the state park decided to close for the season a week before Thanksgiving, we annually count it a blessing that someone discovered the rock castle. Our Thanksgiving home has six bedrooms and two bathrooms with a common kitchen and living space. As babies have arrived on the family scene, the close room proximity means their sleeping patterns affect the entire cabin. But as families do, they forgive, and each morning fight again for a turn to hold the newest member of the Thanksgiving crew.

Uncles, grandparents, cousins, great-grandchildren, sisters of in-laws, across four generations and ties through marriage and friendship, we become the best of friends for five days every November. All are welcome, and once tucked inside for our Thanksgiving retreat, relationships are blurred into one, at least until the annual Turkey Bowl football game.

Throughout our seven years of celebrating Thanksgiving at the cabin, our packing lists have become tighter and our traditions stronger. Turkeys still cook in rock castle kitchens. Southern cornbread stuffing doesn't lose its tastiness, and best of all, an executive decision has been made that the pies can be started on at any time!

And when we pack to leave, at the end of our days of relaxation and family conversations that wouldn't happen unless the timing and location were just right, we climb into those cars that sat still for five days. Our son waves goodbye to the horses, and the crunch of gravel ends as we enter the civilized world of paved roads.

My mind is tempted to begin its 100-mile-an-hour plunge into the whirlwind Christmas season, but it waits. Not wanting the

Thanksgiving refreshment to end, I find Christmas music on the radio and pause. I pause the tranquility of the outdoors, the laughter of good conversation, and the joy of time spent with those I love. And after reflecting on the new Thanksgiving memories, I begin the countdown until next year at the cabin.

JAN UNDERWOOD

It's Not Thanksgiving Until Mommy Cries

MY FAMILY has a long history of dinner-party disasters.

One Thanksgiving, the turkey slipped right off the baking pan as my mother was taking it out of the oven. It slipped and fell with a sickening splop on the linoleum in a big, hot lake of drippings. As I recall, my aunt snagged the bird and put it on a serving platter, and we ate it anyway. Well, what would you have done?

Then there was the time a mouse crawled into the oven and died. My mother had invited her Dean to dinner, and the day was filled, of course, with a frenzy of dusting and vacuuming, of dressing and re-dressing, of chopping and boiling, the fever pitch of Trying to Make a Good Impression by a household that had not had much practice doing that. Some minutes after the lasagna went into the oven, the house was filled with a noxious smell, which turned out to be that of mousie cremation. The lasagna had to be thrown out. In fact, my parents threw the whole stove out. They bought a new one that very

---

Humor writer Jan Underwood writes and teaches in Portland, Oregon, where she lives with her husband and far too many cats. She is the author of one novel, Day Shift Werewolf, *published in 2006 by 3-day Books, and blogs at www.blogatrix.org.*

afternoon, assembled a second lasagna, and salvaged the dinner party, if only just in time.

Then there was the night—another Dean, another party, or perhaps it was all the same dreadful day—when with minutes to spare until the guests arrived, my mother, still unshowered, ordered me to spread sour cream atop the cheesecake. I was ten or eleven at the time. I have no memory of this incident, but my mother reports I knocked on the bathroom door and said, "Mommy? The sour cream looks funny." Frantic, my mother bellowed, "I don't care! Just spread it on!" I did as I was told. Turned out the topping was sour cream with chives.

I don't remember a time when having people to dinner was exempt from high anxiety. My mother went into overdrive; my father went into hiding. I guess in my mother's working-class family, there were no dinner parties. People came to dinner all the time, of course, and there were always enough potatoes in the pot for an extra mouth. But there were no Deans at my grandparents' table; there was no need to be wearing the Right Thing or to sparkle with wit. If you ate at my mother's parents, you were going to eat corned beef and cabbage or chicken, mashed potatoes and canned peas. The house was not from *Sunset* magazine, and the meal was not from *Gourmet*. So my mother had to teach herself those ways, or she felt she had to. When she was at her most ambitious, vaulting herself from the working to the upper-middle class, she put on these affairs as frequently as she could bear and paid for them in gray hairs.

At some point down the line she'd had enough and declared a moratorium on cooking altogether. My father has been the sole cook in their house since the early 1980s. He developed a standard repertoire: Swiss steak one night, roast chicken and Minute Rice with margarine another. In those years we usually had one night each week of fast food and one of scrambled eggs, and one night was dubbed "Every Man for Himself." For my part, I was always content to have a bowl of Frosted Mini-Wheats for dinner.

The menu has evolved with time, of course. And the guest list has as well. The friends who have dinner at my parents' now are just that: friends—people who come for the company, not to have their favor curried. If the chicken is dry or the potatoes unimaginative, what does it matter?

And that's the model of householding and of hosting that I have followed. Dinners, when I make them at all, usually consist of two or three items, scarcely altered from the way they came out of the ground. If I have a visitor, I might put out some hummus and pita bread, and there's always a cup of tea in my kitchen for those who want one. But, comfortable in my class status and utterly un-foodie, I live a life completely and blessedly free of dinner parties.

But.

Some part of me sometimes wants to host Thanksgiving.

Perhaps it's that part of me whose notions about How Things Should Be was shaped in the early days, when there was Deaning and dining in my household. Perhaps it's because I get caught in what my mother, with good reason, calls False Lying Nostalgia. Can I be faulted? The traditional feast day is so heavily wrapped in cultural mythology: the hand-traced construction-paper turkeys, the Norman Rockwell paintings, the warmth of the oven and the wholesome good smells, the companionship that is said to come with the preparations and the pleasures of the dinner table.

At any rate, I wanted Thanksgiving this year. It was the first year of my marriage to Rick. Also, my 19-year-old son moved out in June and hadn't had a home-cooked meal since. Mind you, he didn't have a home-cooked meal prior to that, either. Sam has been looking after his own burritos and single-serve pizzas since he was old enough to operate the microwave. But lately, long-dormant maternal instincts have been yawning and stretching and waking up in me; I have a sense that Sam is growing thin and wan in his bachelor apartment. And Sam was feeling homesick, if only homesick for the kind of Thanksgiving we'd never had.

Looking back, I see that I could have had the whole thing catered, knowing the way stars tend to misalign when Underwoods cook. But I have a certain stubborn desire to do things myself. I feel the same way about sewing fallen buttons back on shirts, painting bedroom walls, growing tomatoes. The truth is I have almost no skill at these kinds of tasks, and I am disinclined to make the effort to learn. But I like the idea of knitting a scarf, making a candle, baking a pie. I like the idea of being the sort of person who does those things. It can't be that hard, I have been known to think. I know I can do this. I think these things, forgetting—or ignoring—a cornucopia of evidence to the contrary.

Early Thanksgiving Day this year, I put the turkey in the sink to thaw. It was only a four-pound breast, so I had left it in the freezer until morning. I made a cranberry sauce according to my whims, which include a notion left over from my quasi-hippie days that cranberry sauce needs no sugar—only a little frozen orange juice concentrate. I had made the sensible decision to think small. No stuffing this year and no sides; no finger-foods, salads or hors d'oeuvres; and certainly no pies. We would satisfy ourselves with the four essentials: turkey, mashed potatoes and gravy, baked yams, and the cranberries.

Rick and I went visiting, which was pleasant, though we came home tired from socializing and wet from walking in the rain. The turkey took longer to baste, and the oven longer to pre-heat, than I had remembered from the last time, whenever that was. I put the bird in to bake 45 minutes late.

Well, what's 45 minutes? Sam came over straight from work, starving but in good cheer. We washed and peeled potatoes together. I don't remember us doing this sort of thing when we were under one roof, but this was what Thanksgiving was about, right? Cheerful kitchen cooperation.

An hour passed. We talked and laughed. Rick lay on the couch and watched TV, hungry but patient. (In his defense, he had a little cold and was feeling puny.) Sam set up our Wi-Fi. We looked at Facebook, we read my blog. Was the turkey done yet? It looked pale, like a fish. Why wasn't it getting brown and filling the house with warm baked-turkey smells? Sam defragged our computer. Our blood sugar was getting low. Thirty, forty minutes more ticked by. Finally, I pulled the turkey out of the oven and cut it open to see what was going on. It was pink and cold inside. Still nearly frozen. Ah. Evidently you have to thaw a turkey the night before it's cooked. At that point we gave up on the meat. We would have potatoes, yams and cranberry sauce for dinner.

We mashed the potatoes, an event that seemed to go smoothly enough. I took the yams out of the oven and poked them with a knife. They were like rocks. Well, this is why God made microwaves. I nuked them two, three, four times until they approximated the texture of proper yams, if a little shriveled on both ends. By now I was coming just a tiny bit unglued. I had saved the turkey drippings, but the prospect of making gravy was now too daunting. To hell with gravy; we would make do.

Rick set the table, sort of. He didn't grow up with dinner parties, either, so we each got a yellow-striped napkin and a plate and a fork. He and Sam drank sparkling cider from the two wine glasses that we own, and I had water in one of those vessels that Pomegranate juice comes in. It's okay, I told myself. We're not proud.

I made a little toast over our carbohydrates, and we tucked in. Not a minute later, Rick was making faces. Dear, sweet Rick. He doesn't have a mean bone in his body. Also, he adheres to the unfortunate belief that honesty is the best policy.

"Why are you grimacing?" I asked.

"The potatoes are undercooked," he said. He couldn't have said, "Oh, nothing, I just bit my tongue," or "Oh, I was just thinking about the Arizona-Arizona State game." No. He told the truth and drove a little ice pick into my heart.

I smiled bravely and asked if anyone had a movie recommendation.

"Mom, you look like you're about to cry," said Sam.

"Really?" I became very interested in the cranberry sauce. Studious, even.

"I have to ask," Rick said from down at his end of the table. "Is this canned gravy?"

I could feel my eyes welling up.

"Mom. You're not really going to cry, are you?"

Soon I was hiding my face in my yellow-striped napkin.

"Don't be sad," they told me. "We don't care."

But I was on a roll, and there was no stopping me now. They patted me while I squeaked, my shoulders shaking with my effort not to make a scene.

By now our little meal of potatoes and dessicated yams was nearly finished. After a pause, Rick said, "Is there any dessert?"

The tears started afresh.

"What can we do to make you feel better?" said Sam.

"The dishes," I sobbed.

"Oh," they said. "That."

We sat a few minutes longer.

"I'm bored," said Sam.

"I'd be willing to clear the table," said Rick. As he gathered up the plates, he mused, "I never have liked cranberries."

I think, now, that it might be time to be done with all this nonsense. To embrace the truth that I cannot cook, and I cannot host, and I do not wish to learn. To let go of the notion that I can nurture my family members in this particular way. Or to expect that the dinner table is a place where they can nurture me. It might be time to let go of Norman Rockwell and paper-doll pilgrims, of recipe exchanges and the image of kitchen comraderie, and of the longing for a past that never was. It might be time to put an end, once and for all, to the family Cooking Curse. Time to free myself at last, and to declare: next Thanksgiving, we're having Frosted Mini-Wheats for dinner.

C. D. JONES

My First Thanksgiving at Home

THANKSGIVING. A day set aside to reflect on what one is thankful for. Having gone to Catholic schools for a number of years, this concept was drilled into me perhaps a bit stronger than that of the average child. For me, a shy, sensitive girl surrounded by the strict, punitive world of both my schooling and my home life, my family was what I was most thankful for. An abnormally strong fear of losing my parents had formed at some point early in my life; hints of sending my sisters and me away when we had misbehaved had perhaps developed this looming fear. At night I lay awake, sleepless, terrified something would happen to my parents that would take them away from me. I felt I could not survive should I lose them.

Flash-forward 35 years. Today I am most thankful that I came down with the flu. Although this may sound absurd, as I lay in bed with my husband, also feverish, my young son, and our dog Rosie, I am as content as one can be. I imagine the Thanksgiving taking place at

---

C. D. Jones lives in the Pacific Northwest with her husband and son. She is a graduate of the University of Washington and is focusing her time on freelance work, writing, spending time with her son and family, and generally feeling overwhelmed.

my parents' home across town, the empty seats witnessing what took years to acknowledge was a highly dysfunctional home. A child's eyes see what they want to see, for they are blessed with endless imagination. Although my parents are now quite old, my time with them limited, I no longer fear losing them as I once did, for they are no longer my core family. I am now blessed with a choice. Family is what surrounds me on this bed. There is no fear, no threats of abandonment. My son will sleep at night.

LISA TROCCHIA-BALKITS

Mangia Mania

Mangi Bene, Ridi Spesso, Ama Molto—Eat Well, Laugh Often, Love Much

—OLD ITALIAN PROVERB

ITALIAN-AMERICANS love to eat. Okay, this might not be established scientifically, but you know it's true. If you have friends or colleagues who are Italian-Americans, you've seen it. If you happen to be Italian-American, you're sure of it. Whether this is due to genetics or is a result of our cultural heritage I do not know, but the truth is we Italian-Americans do love food. We look forward, with almost a perverse anticipation, to any event where good food might be part of the occasion, from a church potluck to a business lunch. (Power lunch? Skip the second martini and throw in another cannoli!) The only thing we might possibly love more than good food is a gathering that combines good food and family. To this day in my family, Thanksgiving is one such occasion. One year, however, events became the stuff of legend to all who experienced it because, well, what happened was simply inconceivable.

It started as most Thanksgivings did. There was nothing unusual about arriving at my grandparent's house, each of us kids, mom and

---

Lisa Trocchia-Balkits is an Italian-American who writes about food and culture from her cabin in the deep woods of Appalachian Ohio.

dad too, carrying nearly our weight in tin-foil-covered plates and baking dishes. Their house was always where we gathered—aunts, uncles, cousins, brothers, sisters—all arriving within minutes of each other and hastily making our way in the door, through the kitchen and down the stairs to the large, finished basement. The faux-wood paneled walls still smelled of Murphy's Oil Soap, the white squares of ceiling tile were dusted free of cobwebs, the carpeted floors vacuumed, and the ping-pong table was transformed, with the help of two extra plywood leaves on either side, into a dinner table for 25. The little kids got card tables squeezed into the available corners of the room, but each small table and the large one was covered in beautiful white linen, set with china, and came complete with a centerpiece and little turkey napkin holders that Grandma had made in a ceramics class.

My grandmother always prepared the turkey, mashed potatoes and gravy. Grandpa made his mother's Sicilian ground meat stuffing with pine nuts, raisins, garlic and Parmesan cheese. It was precisely this blending of American and Italian foods that was the hallmark of the occasion, and as it turned out, was what we suspect did us in.

I think the combining of the two food cultures started because some of the brothers married "American" girls. It was a way to be polite. Back in the day, when my grandfather moved to rural southeastern Ohio to attend Ohio University, he knew what it felt like to be different. Going from Brooklyn to the backwoods in the late 1920s wasn't made all that easy for him, so he forever saw to it that anyone in his home felt welcome to be there. It was that, and the new American daughters-in-law were great cooks in their own Appalachian right. He knew a good thing when he tasted it.

One aunt was renowned for her baked sweet potatoes—the kind that were sticky, golden and dotted with miniature marshmallows on top. She also made some wicked slow-oven baked beans with bacon. I wasn't a huge fan of the green Jell-O with the shredded carrots, but she always brought that, too. Another aunt brought a large pan of cubed bread stuffing and one of cheesy scalloped potatoes all the way from Cleveland, where they had recently moved. My mom, although one of the "Americans," had been part of the family long enough to earn respect for her Eggplant Parmesan, so we always brought that along with her mother's fresh cranberry and orange relish. I think that year, because my grandmother liked it so much, we also brought a small ham.

There was never an occasion, holiday or not, that a meal did not include a massive bowl of rigatoni complete with sauce and meatballs that had cooked for a minimum of two days—anything less was considered "quick sauce." My grandpa insisted on it and was the master chef in that department. For Thanksgiving, Easter and Christmas, he would make some special meatballs with raisins, as well as cook sausage and braciole in the sauce.

Other side dishes found their way to the table, too, possibly some uncle's favorite or things that just couldn't be left out—deviled eggs, coleslaw, beet and onion salad, various cheeses and crackers. Partitioned cut-glass appetizer plates were placed in several strategic places on the table—American ones with sweet gherkins, green olives stuffed with pimiento, carrot and celery sticks with a sour cream dip. Others, the Italian ones, had black olives, prosciutto and melon, salami roll-ups, sweet red roasted peppers and provolone cheese in each compartment. Of course, there was always a large, mixed-green salad as well as fresh-baked rolls and butter.

After we had all been seated and Grace had been said, the passing of the food was in itself a bit of magic. Things would always start being passed politely to the left but ended up coming at you from every direction. Time was of the essence because the thing was, we were all starving and no one would dare eat before every dish had been passed to every person, and the plates began to assume a distinctive vertical aspect.

So this is how things started on that Thanksgiving, like many before and after, and it was a wonderful afternoon of much talk, much laughter, and many repeated "yum" sounds, compliments and, being Italian-Americans, good-hearted criticism as well. "Ellen, the baked beans are delicious, but maybe a bit more bacon next time, eh?" "Who brought the deviled eggs? Carol? I like them better without mustard!"

Dessert followed, unbelievably, in short order. There was coffee first, but of course, that was prepared downstairs close to the action, so most adults at the table did not rise after having been seated, literally, for hours. My mom was the dessert queen; her pumpkin pie with whipped cream, with a crust so light it melted in your mouth, was the Thanksgiving ultimate. And then there were her large, overstuffed cream puffs. You also had to save room for Grandma's specialty, the blackberry cake with chocolate fudge icing. There was also custard pie, cannoli, Italian cookies of all kinds, banana nut bread, fudge, Jell-O, and fresh fruit. At that point, it became for me, and most everyone else at the table except my diabetic great aunt, who managed to sit gracefully with a cup of coffee, a complete sweet transcendence. Of course, the children could only tolerate so much sitting, unlimited access to sweets or not. Eventually we were released to play outside, but only after formally asking my grandfather, "May I be excused, please?"

I had just finished my last bite of pumpkin pie—my second "sliver," I think—was excused from the table and eager to go outside and play with my cousins. I bounded up the stairs from the basement into the kitchen, and something happened to catch my eye. Grandmother had recently gotten a new stove—it was avocado green and the kind with a window in the oven door and a light that could be turned on to watch things bake. I was always the kid who hung around in the kitchen. I loved watching food being made, and this new advantage of peering into the oven while things were cooking I found fascinating, so I always looked into the oven when I went by. It was just curiosity and a habit I still have. What I saw then, however, made me stop in my tracks.

That year, more than two-and-a-half hours after Thanksgiving dinner had started, adults still sitting around the table, pushed back in their chairs, belts loosened a notch or two, and last coffees being finished, I realized that the turkey was still in the oven. What kind of madness was this? I yelled for my mother and after that, all I can remember is deafening laughter. Were we all victims of some kind of hysterical, food-induced mass delusion? Can you imagine a Thanksgiving dinner with so much food that not one person—man, woman or child—missed the turkey? Well, it is a true story, and all I can say for sure is, being Italian-Americans, we were already looking forward to turkey and meatball sandwiches the next day!

CAROL J. RHODES

Omi's Turkey & Dressing

ON THE DAY BEFORE Thanksgiving, as far back as I can remember, my mother and grandmother would get together and perform an execution. They would don rubber gloves, old clothes and shoes (or boots if it was muddy), and head for the barnyard.

A fire was started under an old wash pot, water from the cistern was heated, and the axe sharpened. The victim, chosen well in advance, was removed from his cage and brought to the stump of an old tree. There were no glaring lights, no television cameras, no reporters—only the early morning sun peeking through the trees, and me, peeking between the fingers of my hands, which I held firmly against my face.

Designated as Helper, it was my mother's job to hold the victim in place—no small task if you have ever witnessed a turkey who didn't want to be dinner. My grandmother, working under the title of Butcher, wielded the death blow. After the reflex action of the body had stopped, the turkey was picked up by the legs and plunged into

---

Carol J. Rhodes' creative work—short stories, essays, poetry, plays, and nonfiction articles—has been widely published, appearing in newspapers, magazines, journals, anthologies, and books, including Chicken Soup for the Girlfriend's Soul. She is also a freelance literary and technical editor, and instructor of business writing courses, "Why Not Write it Right?" and "Email Protocol."

the scalding water. Afterwards, its feathers were plucked and saved in an old pillowcase, for what later use I don't know, while the legs and intestines were removed and tossed to two old dogs who showed little or no enthusiasm in being so honored.

Once the bird was brought into the kitchen, the executioners changed into clean clothes and shoes and donned crisp, bib-type aprons. It was then they were magically transformed into Cordon Bleu chefs. With deft hands, the turkey was stuffed with dressing prepared from an old German recipe, then trussed, slathered in melted butter, and baked to a beautiful golden brown.

After my grandmother died, my mother worked primarily alone in the preparation of Thanksgiving dinner, even though I was now supposed to be the Helper. With our turkeys coming from the supermarket these days, we both concluded that watching a turkey being thawed, as opposed to being killed, was a whole lot easier.

The first Thanksgiving after my mother died, I studied her recipe for turkey and dressing for days before attempting to follow in her footsteps. Finally, I felt I was ready. In my grandmother's apron, I sliced, diced, simmered, stirred, toasted, roasted, and basted. During dinner, I knew my efforts had somewhat paid off when my young son said, "Mom, this turkey tastes just like Omi's." I suddenly felt a large lump in my throat as tears rolled down my cheeks. Since then, it has taken many years to perfect these techniques so that preparation does not take a whole week.

Now when I am invited to the home of one of my children for a holiday dinner, it always begins with, "Mom, we'll fix everything else, but would you please do the turkey and dressing? No one else's is as good as yours." I always agree to the trade, since I consider it a much simpler task than tidying the house, polishing silver, washing china and crystal, pressing linens, and the inevitable cleaning up afterwards.

OLIVIA ANNE CAFFREY

Bird is the Word—A Long Island Thanksgiving Memory

THERE IS AN EIGHT-HOUR, slightly hellish trip to purgatory/"heaven is what you make of it."

I get to bond with my sister. So much has changed since I last saw the devil when she helped me move on September 1. She is cutting down on her shopping addiction because of the "potential looming financial crisis." She bought a bed with four mattresses. She has changed the way she applies eyeliner. She read both bestsellers *The Kite Runner* and *A Thousand Splendid Suns* by Khaled Hosseini. I think my sister has finally discovered reading, and I want to cry for joy. We talk as sisters should and it's been way too long since we've done that. We sleep in her bed together peacefully; two overgrown products of my strange parents' sex life.

Erin leaves for Calgary, Canada, to be with her Canadian boyfriend for "Thanksgiving."

Olivia Caffrey is a teacher, brewer, and writer. Olivia grew up on Long Island and moved to Boston. She has worked as an editorial assistant for the Weekly Dig, *and freelanced for* What's Up? Magazine. *Olivia Caffrey is interested in all things food and what it means to be grateful.*

My parents and I eat good New York pizza. I answer a few Jeopardy questions correctly and my mom is convinced that I am a genius. My attempt to make vegan cookies is Plaster-of-Paris.

"Bird is the Word."

The next day my mom and I are on the verge of a thousand splendid fights, but I realize it's all in my head. Phil's cranberry sauce is made. The festive corduroys are ironed. The threats of sudden death if we don't leave for Grandma's house on time are forgotten with the bizarrely warm weather.

"Mom, can I drive, please?"

"No, Thanksgiving is a crazy driving day!"

I am 27 years old and trying to get my driver's license.

At the Daly's, we eat turkey; my dad carves. He also carves his finger a bit, and I later give him a Jesus band-aid that the Catholic schoolboy in him just loves. This Long Island feast includes: canned green beans, sweet potatoes with marshmallows, creamed canned onions, Pillsbury dough boy pop-in fresh muffins, fresh rolls, Italian bread, canned asparagus, canned olives, canned corn, canned carrots, celery with cream cheese, boxed mashed potatoes, canned cranberry sauce, Phil's real cranberry sauce with orange juice, home-made stuffed shells with spinach, Costco lasagna, stuffing from a box, oh yeah, and two turkeys! One untouched! This Thanksgiving meal, much of it from a can, is classic for me. It's a part of my American working-class Thanksgiving understanding and it's so scrumptilicious...

Danny, the last of the crew, and me, the first and best (ha!) rake leaves into a giant pile for jumping purposes. I cousin-pressure 16-year-old shy bombshell Lauren, explaining that this leaf fun is like a "kid-friendly version of MTV's *Jackass*" and she jumps. Danny jumps into the leaves with her whole body like a little wood nymph; the leaves cushion her like a rusty photosynthesis cloud. I do a log roll into the leaves and my bones crush a little on the earth. I do a tumblesault. But the most fun is the home-run slide—you take off your shoes, get a running start, and fall, fall, oh so suddenly and oh so fast...

We all watch home videos and crack jokes on how stupid and totally adorable the kids were as babies. We take turns embarrassing different cousins and ask them to do the stupid, adorable things they are doing in the video as babies, such as drooling, losing control of facial muscles, and making strange beastly noises under tables. It is so strange seeing your melancholy, 14-year-old self speaking on video. Who says there is no such thing as a time machine?

All the men and boys silently play Texas Hold 'Em. All the kids get a little cash from my grandparents' monthly Atlantic City trip. My grandmother knows about and loves football as she bets money on it. The Jets commit suicide on TV while live karaoke blares in the other room. Catherine and I do a slightly rousing version of "Rolling Down the River" and score a B+. We sing a few songs as a group, and we are so horribly off-key, off-beat, and off-sync that it is not even funny. But, now that I am older, I just close my eyes, say a secular Grace, take a sip, and it kind of makes sense. Uncle Mike sings several songs and so does Grandpa—they both are doing their best Frank Sinatra. My grandpa, a man of few words and much back pain, takes his lounge act seriously. And you've got to respect a man that used to be chief of the fire department and that fancies he used to look like Elvis Presley.

The kids and I play several energetic rounds of Hide and Scare. The hider's job is to scare the shit out of the seekers, my idea. We do our best imitations of each other, nearly pissing our pants. Big Chris says he has not laughed like this in a long time. In doses, I think it's good fun, too.

My parents and I talk about everybody on the way home, in a rare cordial way. We talk of the bumps-on-the-logs, the complainers, the princesses, the losers, the liars, the overweight, the sad, and the overachievers, and how we had a pretty nice time with them, and how, in a way, we are they.

Most years we just fight or are awkwardly silent on the way home from Thanksgiving.

It's always curious to break tradition.

In the Camry, I hear 1963's "Surfin' Bird" by The Trashmen. Right then it sounds so awesome—

"Bbbbbbbbbbbbbbbbb . . . [retching noises] . . . aaah!
Pa-pa-pa-pa-pa-pa-pa-pa-pa-pa-pa-pa-pa-pa-pa-pa

Pa-pa-pa-pa-pa-pa-pa-pa-pa-pa-pa-pa-pa-pa-ooma-mow-mow
Well, don't you know about the bird
Well, everybody knows that the bird is the word
A-well-a, bird, bird, b-bird's the word."

We get home and my mom gives me suede cowboy boots, then the three of us watch the end of *The Birds*. My dad says that after tonight's attractions, not only will we never want to eat a turkey again, but we will also never want to take a shower. We start to watch *Psycho* on the wrap-around couch, except my parents fall asleep and go to bed before it's over...

SHERYL L. NELMS

Thanksgiving is

the fat pop of
boiling cranberries

cornbread dressing and turkey gravy
pumpkin pie piled with whipped cream

frost on the windshield

pheasant hunting
deer tracks in green wheat
flocks of migrating geese honking overhead

the scent of a mesquite
wood fire in the Franklin stove

football and spiced cider

our nondenominational
interracial

diversity day of appreciation
for another
chance

Sheryl L. Nelms is from Marysville, Kansas. She graduated from South Dakota State University with a degree in Family Relations and Child Development. She has had over 5,000 articles, stories and poems published, including 14 individual collections of her work. She is the Fiction and Nonfiction Editor of the Pen Woman *magazine, the publication of the National League of American Pen Women.*

LOREN STEPHENS

Thanksgiving Obituary

IT WAS TOUCH-AND-GO if we would even have a Thanksgiving dinner. Karen's mother was on life support and Karen was not up to cooking, so everything other than my potato-leek Gruyère side dish was store-bought at Gelson's. The kitchen counter was covered with Styrofoam containers and Saran-wrapped platters. The welcoming smell of roasting turkey and bubbling gravy were sadly missing.

Karen's Swedish houseguests, Birgitta and Sven, and I watched the blazing sun dropping down into the Pacific Ocean, leaving pink-orange clouds in its wake. As darkness descended, and neighborhood Christmas lights were turned on, we listened for the telephone to ring giving us an update on Karen's estimated return from the hospital. To avoid picking at the turkey, we served the tomato crostini hors d'oeuvres. Karen's father dropped a cracker, face down, on her pristine white carpet, leaving a blood-red stain, which I tried to wipe out before Karen came home.

At 7:30, Karen called to say that her mother would not let go of her hand and so she would stay until the latest round of painkillers

---

Loren Stephens is the founder of Write Wisdom and Provenance Press, which provide memoir writing and publishing services. She teaches a course titled "Writing Memoir." Formerly an Emmy-nominated filmmaker, her personal essays have appeared in Distillery, MacGuffin, Jewish Women's Literary Annual, Oracle, The Los Angeles Times, Chicago Tribune, Sun Magazine, Tapestries *and other publications.*

kicked in and she fell asleep. We decided to put out the meal and eat. Karen's father, 98, was showing signs of fatigue, and all of us were hungry despite the sadness of the occasion. We had more or less finished our meal when Karen came home from the hospital. Thankfully she spared us the details of her mother's condition, although the telephone rang, and we could hear her discussing "end of life" options with family members living in Ohio who had experience with these situations.

This was not the Thanksgiving that we all had looked forward to, and hardly resembled past occasions together over ten years with Karen's mother and father bringing homemade cranberry sauce or chestnut soup to our house. Every year the guests around the table changed, but Karen and her parents were a constant and thought of my husband and me as part of their extended family. Her mother, Eva, was model-thin with high cheekbones and a gracious manner, always interested in what everyone was doing with their lives. Her father was a courtly gentleman, madly in love with his wife, with stories to share about life in Columbus, Ohio, before the war—World War II.

It was our familiarity with one another that made the decision to have a Thanksgiving dinner palatable. Karen said, "Let's just keep it low key. I know that I don't have to put on a happy face, but it will be comforting to have you over." And that is what Thanksgiving should be—a gathering of close friends who are there for one another, and with whom much is said through silence.

Two days later, Eva passed away. Karen asked me if I would write her mother's obituary. The weather had changed; it was raining hard, so I drove slowly down Montana Avenue to the assisted living facility where her mother and father had spent the past three years as popular residents. One of the attendants rang the doorbell of their little apartment to say how much she would miss Karen's mother. "She was always so kind and generous to me. She was one of the most popular ladies here. So sorry."

I brought a copy of the day's *New York Times* obituary section to show examples of various family tributes, which helped focus our efforts. How to encapsulate a life in a few short paragraphs? I made some suggestions and the ideas started coming. I learned a lot about

Karen's mother—that she had been a champion swimmer and bowler, and an enthusiastic volunteer for a number of charities, including reading to children, something that I did on a regular basis with children in the Los Angeles Unified public schools. Karen wanted to be sure that we included her mother's motto, "Don't get. Just give." And what about flowers? No, in lieu of flowers, please make a contribution to a charity of your choice for the benefit of children.

The antique clock on the wall chimed and suddenly I could hardly breathe. I felt my throat constrict and a pain in my chest expand through my ribs and lungs. I did not want to say anything, but I knew I was having a panic attack. Writing Karen's mother's obituary brought up the loss I went through when my own mother passed away five years before, and I was the "designated writer" with my sister of the obituary that ended up in *The New York Times*.

I remember my sister pitching me a line, "And she threw a mean dinner party." That didn't make the final cut, but we proceeded to do a lengthy riff on my mother's lack of culinary skills. She had a few standard recipes: Greek egg drop soup, *bouef a la mode* and raspberry parfait. Thanksgiving was outside her repertoire. She relied on our maid and cook to assemble our family dinners, which coincided with my father's birthday, November 26.

We always had my father's favorite cake—a chocolate-covered jelly roll. He'd blow out the candles and then we'd go skating on our pond if the ice was thick enough. Sometimes we even had a snowstorm, which shrank the number of family members down to just a few who lived nearby. It had been a long time since I thought of those Thanksgiving celebrations. My father died at the age of 52, some 40 years ago.

Karen's mother was 93. From my vantage point, a good long life, well lived with a loving husband still around to care for her until the end and a devoted daughter. Much to be thankful for.

MARIANNE LONSDALE

Passing the Turkey

First Down

I wasn't sure how Mom would react to my offer to take over Thanksgiving dinner. When my six brothers, my sister, and I congregated with spouses and kids, we numbered about 30 hearty eaters. Mom was 70 years old. Thanksgiving was the only holiday she still hosted. Would she be insulted? Feeling a little nervous, I called her in September.

"I'm not sure if you'd like this," I started. "So just say no if you don't want this to happen." I tend to waver with my mom between apologizing unnecessarily and steamrolling over her. "I'd be interested in hosting Thanksgiving."

"Oh, that would be great." Relief flooded Mom's voice. "Thanksgiving is really too much for me to handle. It has been for a long time. But none of you kids seemed to want to do it."

Whew. That was great—she was happy and I was happy. Why hadn't she just told us she didn't want to host? Letting go wasn't always easy for Mom.

Marianne Lonsdale lives with her husband, Michael, and son, Nicholas, in Oakland, California. She is a member of the Writing Mama Salon at Book Passage in Corte Madera, and her writing mentor is Charlotte Cook, a writer, teacher, and publisher.

"Your father will be so pleased." She always punted to Dad; ultimately any decision had to do with making him happy.

She called me in early November.

"Would you like me to make the spinach casserole?" she asked. "I could bring two. You know how your brothers eat."

Two packs of frozen spinach, one can of cream of potato soup, an eight-ounce container of sour cream, one-quarter cup parmesan cheese. Mix all ingredients together, top with Monterey Jack cheese and bake for 30 minutes. This glop didn't work with our menu.

"We're not serving the spinach casserole." Best to just tell her the truth, get it over with.

"No spinach casserole?" Mom queried. "Is that what you said?" Shock and denial could be heard. Darn, maybe I should have eased into letting her know we'd axed this family heirloom.

My husband, Michael, and I had come up with our own Thanksgiving menu. The spinach casserole was a relic from the 70s that needed retirement. I'd introduced the dish to the family, so I thought I could be the one to say goodbye.

"We're going to sauté fresh green beans with garlic, olive oil and toasted slivered almonds," I said. Maybe I was moving too fast, maybe menu changes were a foul play in the first year.

"I see," Mom said, which meant she didn't. "Is it okay if I bring creamed onions? Do you still like those?"

"Super," I nearly shouted. My overly enthusiastic response sounded like a kindergarten teacher encouraging a five-year-old.

Well, this Thanksgiving would be at my house. I should be able to make a few changes. Would she notice that we'd ditched the monster whip? That sweet mass of green Jell-O mixed with Cool Whip and pineapple chunks? My teeth ached thinking about it.

I thought I knew my boundaries. My father could not be deprived of his cylinder of canned cranberry sauce. I would also serve my homemade cranberry ginger chutney and hope to convert him.

Nineteen of us squeezed into our small house that first year. Although I missed those unable to come, I was grateful not to be cooking for all 30. We added three leaves to the dining room table, but still needed nine spots. Like my mom, I set up a table and chairs in the living room.

Logistics were complicated. Our kitchen has one small oven. We surveyed our neighbors to find out who would be gone and snagged an extra kitchen. My mother, like a proud lioness, stood at my front door, arms crossed, smiling and nodding as she watched me, two of her sons, and two grandchildren parade with covered side dishes across the street, up steep stone steps and into the borrowed kitchen.

I wasn't sure what prayer, what toast, what blessing, I'd give before the meal. I'm not religious, but I like ritual and was moved by having my family at my home. We stood gathered around the two tables, hand in hand, and I was about to ad lib, to see what rose from heart to mind.

"Corky, please say grace," my mother said to my sister-in-law. Corky, a devout Christian, often led the family in prayer.

My mouth and throat almost interrupted. I'm here. This is my house. I think I have something to say. But I stifled my words. Change can be hard, even when it's in the right direction. My mother, the matriarch for so many years, had earned holding rights.

Incomplete Pass

Mom and I planned on the telephone for my second year of hosting.

"Anything else I can bring?" she asked. "What else can I do to help?"

"Everyone will be here this year," I explained. I had to work the day before Thanksgiving and was feeling a bit desperate for help. "If you could get here a couple of hours early, I'd have you help set the tables and mash the potatoes. Say, about 2:00?"

"Well, since we're not eating until 4:00, your father and I will arrive about 3:00. That should be plenty of time."

Thanks for asking, Mom. She was gonna do what she was gonna do. She was a pro at turnovers, asking what I needed even though she had no intention of changing her game plan.

My sister-in-law, Corky, and I stood in the kitchen that Thanksgiving, debating the pros and cons of mashing potatoes with an electric mixer. Would quality be sacrificed for speed? My mother hovered on the other side of the room.

"I'd make a suggestion, but no one ever listens to mine," she muttered loud enough for me to hear.

I ignored her but felt a twinge of guilt. I wasn't listening to her, and I had no idea what suggestions I'd ignored. But my annoyance at her refusal to do things my way pushed the guilt aside. This was my house after all.

I said the first grace that day. My family stood around my dining room table and stretched hands across to the living room, set with two rented tables and chairs. I was moved to tears by the sight of all of us, so grown up, living, working and loving in ways we hadn't foreseen. I spoke of my gratefulness for the joy of our children, of this next generation. My tears stopped my words short of all I wanted to say but that was okay. I'd let some of my emotions spill out to my family.

After dinner I lined up each family member, one by one, in front of the fireplace to take pictures. A few years had passed since we had all been together at my parents' 50th wedding anniversary. I wanted to capture us at this point in time.

My mother and father, who started us all. Jim and his partner, Lamar. My sister, Cathy, and her teenage daughter, Juliane. My brother, Matt, and his three kids. I still missed his ex-wife, Tracy. Joe, Corky and their six kids—one in a wheelchair. Pat, Andrea and baby Tori, visiting from Texas. Vin, Yang and their two beautiful babies. Me with Michael and Nick. Don, my baby brother, now 34.

Then I grouped myself with all my siblings. I wanted a picture of us, of my generation.

"You need us in there," my mother said. She rose from her chair, tugging my father's hand.

"We'll take one with you and Dad next," I said.

"Don't you want us in this one?" she asked.

"Next," I said. "I want one of just the kids, and then one with you and Dad."

Seemed reasonable to me but Mom was chomping at the bit to get in the frame. The pictures sit in a small album on my piano today. I gave each family an album for Christmas. My mom carried hers with her for months, pulling it out of her purse to show friends her beautiful family whenever she had a chance.

Fumbling to the Finish

"How about if I bring some brussel sprouts?" Mom suggested the next year. "I know Michael likes them."

"That's okay," I responded. "We're having the green beans almandine again. Besides, I don't think anyone except Michael would eat the brussel sprouts."

Why couldn't I just let her bring them? Sometimes I get so stuck on doing things my way that I don't let my mother come to the table. I continue to punish her for childhood slights even though I'm almost 50. On the other hand, why won't she just let me be in charge of things at my own house?

"Okay, dear," Mom said. "I just thought Michael would enjoy brussel sprouts. I leave tomorrow for my hiking trip with the girls. See you on Thanksgiving."

Mom strode into the kitchen on Thanksgiving with a covered casserole dish. Bigger than the one she brings the creamed onions in. Dad followed. He carried the creamed onion dish.

"Michael, I made brussel sprouts for you," she called out, even before saying hello.

"Great," my ever-gracious husband responded.

We had Thanksgiving routines now. Tables rented on Wednesday. Michael prepared the turkey, stuffing and gravy. I shopped, set the tables, cooked the sweet potatoes, green beans, cranberry sauces and mashed potatoes. The grandkids eagerly lined up to be part of the parade of side dishes to our neighbor's kitchen. Turkey day had nearly shifted to my house.

My husband sat at the head of the table. I sat to his left, in the chair closest to the kitchen. My mother sat across from me. Michael spooned some brussel sprouts onto his plate. The sprouts looked good. Mom had chopped them into small leaves and steamed them in chicken broth.

I took a small serving and passed the dish to my left. Each person at the table passed the brussel sprouts without taking any until they reached my mother. She scooped some leaves on her plate.

"Mmmm," she said. "Do you like the brussel sprouts, Michael?"

"Yes," Michael answered. "Tasty."

"How I got them is a funny story," Mom said. "On our way to Yosemite, the girls and I stopped at a produce stand. The stand had fresh brussel sprouts, still on the stalk."

Michael nodded, chewing on the brussel sprouts.

"But I didn't buy them then. I didn't want to drag them around all week. I figured I'd pick them up on the way home."

Mom had a funny smirk going on.

"Well, we stop at the same produce stand on Sunday," Mom continued. "And no brussel sprouts. I was so disappointed."

"So did you end up buying these at Safeway?" I asked.

"No, here's the funny part," she said. "I tell the man working at the produce stand that I had seen terrific-looking brussel sprouts just five days earlier. He explains that those sprouts had started turning bad and he had thrown them in the dumpster just that morning."

She looked at Michael. She'd emphasized "just that morning." To Mom, that phrase was the same as saying "fresh." I knew where this story was going, but Michael hadn't caught on yet.

"So he let me take them from the dumpster," she explained. "And I cooked them this morning. Lucky save, huh?"

Michael put his fork down. Stalled for time by wiping his mouth with his napkin.

"Fresh from the dumpster five days ago?" he joked.

"Yes, and they taste great, don't they?" Mom said. "And the kicker is the man didn't even charge me."

She was so pleased with her resourcefulness. I couldn't burst her bubble. I pushed the sprouts around on my plate but didn't eat any.

I'm more like my mom than I care to admit. We both get fixed on certain ways of doing things, and we both steamroll over each other's suggestions. I am so grateful on Thanksgiving that I still have my mom. I need to find more for her to do than just pass the turkey.

EMILY PEPIN

Returning

TWO DAYS before Thanksgiving. Train headed north, direction of Canada and Vikings. Albuquerque to Santa Fe. En route, like the past six months. My feet rest on the opposite chair. The green and black backpack takes up an entire seat by itself. It's ripping at the bottom and the top and at the seam of the right strap. I mended it poorly with duct tape and safety pins before leaving Paris. The music of MGMT flows through my headphones: *Yeah, it's overwhelming, but what else can we do, get jobs with offices and wake up for the morning news?* The song is a closed-off secret made for me, a head-sized room of silence (because sometimes silence isn't made by an absence of noise inside but by the absence inside of the outside noise).

The "RailRunner Commuter Train" (called that so people won't expect it to run throughout the day) rushes past New Mexico's martian landscape. Sky more electric blue than I remember. Horizon more austere. Mountain, hill, flatland, highway. The view looks like it will outlast you because it will.

These hills are Mounds of Earth. Streaking their dirt across the sky when the wind kicks up. Cold today. Dustdevils. Green scrubs

---

Emily Pepin graduated from the Johnston Center for Integrative Studies at the University of Redlands in May 2009 with a self-designed emphasis in "Writing Human Ecology." She currently lives in Santa Fe, New Mexico, where she successfully surprised her family for Thanksgiving in November 2009.

clutch the hills. Slopes and steep edges, rising up like fingers out of flatlands. *Mesa.* Mountain. Juniper. *Pinon.* Grasses dance across the valleys looking the way a parched mouth feels. The train passes the ruddy pueblos, looking themselves like natural formations. An overhead announcement comes on: *Please respect the privacy of the Native Americans and refrain from taking pictures.* When the doors open and close, a sound like a railrunner chirp goes off repeatedly, aggravating my hangover. I curse yesterday's Irish car bombs.

No one drinks Irish car bombs in Ireland. But if they did, I bet they wouldn't call them that.

It is two days before Thanksgiving. Holiday of cross-cultural feasting. Holiday of deception—how do Native Americans celebrate it?

Small-pox holiday. Invasion holiday. Holiday where they actually ate eel instead of turkey. Jolly, roly-poly Americans enjoying their roly-poly holiday, football (which isn't really football in the rest of the world) and all.

Thanksgiving. Giving thanks. Thanks to be given. To give thanks. Thanks you give. Thanks for giving. Thanks for thanking. Thinking of thanks. Thanks for keeping the Pilgrims from starving, thanks be to God, Puritanical, Christian God. Thanks be to America and her bountiful bread basket, corn subsidies and corporate stockyards.

Harvest holiday. Holiday celebrating our collective obesity.

Two days and it will be over. I'll have done what I said I would do.

I met a German who told me Thanksgiving is the most important holiday for families in the United States. I suppose it's true—unlike most of our celebrations, the only gifts you receive are a good meal and the company you keep.

I remember the Thanksgivings of my childhood in the suburbs of New York. Aunt Judy and Uncle Paul's. The smell of damp leaves and earth, the ground alive with fire colors, wisps of my hair forming a halo around my flushed face. Each breath visible in the air. I wore special-occasion dresses in reds and oranges, thick tights, Mary Janes.

I don't remember the food. Only playing catch with my father and sister after dinner, or walking to the edge of the yard and feeling like I had traveled very, very far. I remember a golden fawn statue that was about my height, how I loved to play with the hourglass in the living room. The sight of corduroy and my grandmother's pale hands.

Two days before the holiday they don't know I'll be home for. I've forgotten what I imagined it will be like to surprise them. I've forgotten if I had a plan for how I would do it. I can't conjure up an image of how each of them will react. Maybe I've forgotten their faces, maybe they've forgotten mine. Maybe when they see me they'll want to rearrange me, fix my hair. I don't know. How long does it take for us to become strange to our own family?

That's a joke. We're strange to our families all our lives.

Two days until Thanksgiving, and it's hard for me to feel it because all I am busy begging my brain to forget is how close he is, because he is so far away. Santa Fe. Barcelona. The simple truth of simple words: *I may never see you ever again.*

Two days before Thanksgiving.

What are you thankful for about this *life that you are* returning *to?*

The sound of Joni Mitchell and the smell of coffee in the kitchen when I wake up. My mother's art projects scattered throughout the house. My sister's loud laugh, clear as church bells. The arroyo near the house where we walk the dogs. That I have the father all fathers should be. Yoga. The Beatles... my period... sunsets, my five senses, Zoey the poodle, friends, trains, feet, socks, mobility, cannibis, hammocks, Brazil, the entire trip through Europe, my college degree, California, my citizenship, Ben & Jerry's New York Super Fudge Chunk, the environmental justice movement. I try to fill my brain with bits of thankfulness and remembering, so that it will have no vacant space.

Of course, that never works.

I suppose it's possible to love quickly and much, and then to let it fall out of your body like it's loose change, and like your heart is a pants pocket with a hole in the bottom.

Something to remember and be grateful for: *How good it is that things like this exist, not in spite of the hurt, but because of it.*

He'd like the lined look of this high-desert country, land that shows its wear and tear. The same way his face does when he smiles. Harsh and unrelentingly raw and impossible. The most beautiful thing I have ever seen.

Two days until the best meal of my life. After budgeting money and minute portions, I am facing the greatest meal that has ever been and will ever be. If I were to rule the day, I would make it so that only my mother would ever cook it, and only I would ever eat it, because only she can do it right, and only I can know how good it tastes, just as only she can be my mother and only I can be her daughter.

I want yams, big piles of yams with cinnamon dusting and pecans crunched on top, butter and sugar melting into grainy orange. I want chilled apple cider and champagne, green beans with fried onions on top, the Campbell's cream of mushroom soup recipe. I want the tantalizing aroma of paprika-salt-and-pepper turkey to fill my nostrils in our too-small kitchen with the sunflower trim on the floor and the windows where my parents religiously watch birds in the backyard. I want my father's mashed potatoes and the debate that ensues over the proper quantity of salt. I want to drench everything in gravy, and I want cranberry sauce at the table, but only if it's from a can—not because I eat it but because I love how it looks—cyber-age food coming to meet our nation's oldest holiday.

I want stuffing. My god, do I want stuffing.

I want to hold my full belly in my hands and not suck it in, not ever care how fat my ass gets and have Thanksgiving dinner for hours, picking at the ends of the meal and avoiding the dishes by sitting at the kitchen table that, on its underside, still bears the mark of drawings my sister and I made in crayon when we were little. I want us to go around in a circle and have everyone say what we're thankful for: *Cats*, my cousin will say. *My family*, my mother will say. *Indoor plumbing*, my father will say. *Self-sufficiency*, my sister will say. *The sun*, my aunt will say. *Hands*, my sister's girlfriend will say. *Romanticism*, I will say.

I want to feel like my insides have stopped churning because I am settled in the right place. I want to feel heavy, like a tree in its roots.

Two days before Thanksgiving and so close to home, it aches.

Home. I tasted the word on my tongue many times while I was away. Uttered it, chanted it into being, willed myself to become the word, over and over again, breathing deep, trying to send waves of light to 23 Alcalde Road to form a force field around it until I got back. I wanted a promise that it would remain just so, a guarantee that it would not be harmed. Home. *Only say the word and ye shall be healed.*

I had a very scary night in late October with a 56-year old man. We were alone in his cabin in the Haute-Pyrenees, on the very tip of Southern France, the first Basque house of Spain visible from his garden, where I worked in exchange for room and board. That night he didn't take me back down the mountain to my apartment. He tried to touch me in ways only lovers are permitted and to convince me I was pregnant. He was at the end of his rope with his marriage and told me I could heal him. He took hits of LSD and his eyes were like globes boring into mine. I petted his white kitten in the cabin and tried to keep my stare locked on his so he would know I was brave and unafraid, which I am not, and I was. I had no way of escape, and so I slept beside him in the loft. At some point in the night I left the cabin to go to the outhouse. I stepped outside and stared into a black sea filled with floating stars. The Pyrenees loomed. A few hot tears flowed down my frozen face. *Home.*

The next day I wrote the word big in my notebook, pressing the pen down hard. I whispered it into my pillow. Please, dear universe, I know you have already been too good to me, I know we are, and could be, and shall be and have to be, and are born to be, our own beings living beyond our physical dwelling places but please.

Please.

Keep it safe. Bring me safely back.

It is two days before Thanksgiving, and I have forgotten everything about my country. I have forgotten the enormity of SUVs, the grating sound of commercials on the radio, the normalcy of devoting entire aisles in huge grocery stores to salad dressing. I have forgotten that you can't drink alcohol on the street and the accent of mid-westerners; I have forgotten the faces of my family, and roads and language and friendships, and all manner of people.

But. But. Something in me remembers. I can tell. I cradle Walt Whitman's *Leaves of Grass* in my hands and can almost hear the song of myself. Bruce Springsteen is in my headphones. I see the wood walls of my room when I close my eyes. I feel my bones and blood bound by this country, one small part of a hearty, bold, bright and enormous nation.

I know that we are united by our common enthusiasm and our patchwork genetics. I know why I left, and why I was afraid to leave, and why I chose to come back. I am vividly aware that it is two days before Thanksgiving, and I am alive and in the United States once more, and that this holiday is our country's and no others, and for that I am proud and glad, so glad, to be a part of it.

Two days before Thanksgiving. The train is pulling into downtown Santa Fe. I am saying to the universe: *Thank you. Thank you. Thank you.*

BARBARA BOOTHE LOYD

Turkey in Crust

WHEN I MARRIED at age 19, I assumed cooking would be easy if I used our practical wedding gift, the *Better Homes & Gardens Cookbook*. My older sister learned to cook, but for some reason my mother only allowed me to wash and dry dishes. I found reading cookbooks exciting after I married. No dish seemed too complicated to try. Soon, I graduated from just using the BH&G to clipping out recipes from the Washington Post. A few weeks before Thanksgiving, I spotted a fascinating one, "Turkey in Crust," and decided to try it for the upcoming holiday.

We knew several other couples among our circle of Army friends who would also be away from their homes during the holiday. A potluck Thanksgiving dinner was planned. I made invitations and mailed them out. We were responsible for preparing the turkey, and the other dishes were to be brought by our guests. One G.I. volunteered to bring a dish his mother made, Scalloped Corn.

We purchased our turkey at the commissary. Directions for thawing safely were followed precisely. The recipe for the dough seemed easy as I assembled the ingredients. Enough pastry to cover a medium-sized turkey required two bowls filled with flour, salt, baking

---

Barbara Boothe Loyd grew up in Sweetwater, Texas. Literature and art history were her majors at the University of Maryland. She taught art and English for 20 years. She and her husband presently live in Tulsa, Oklahoma, where she volunteers as a docent at the Philbrook Museum of Art.

powder and water. Luckily, I had bowls suitable for the task. I stirred and kneaded as the recipe indicated, and eventually had a product to be proud of. The next step required some ingenuity. Our kitchen was so small, I had to clear off everything from the countertop to accommodate the huge amount of dough to be rolled out. But this, too, was accomplished.

The bird was eventually positioned in the middle of this field of dough and carefully covered by overlapping and tucking edges moistened with water to allow a seamless pastry. I read the recipe once more before popping the bird into the oven and pierced the flour-based covering in several places to allow moisture to escape during the baking process.

The 350 degree oven began its work. Eventually, luscious smells of baking turkey filled our little apartment the day of our party. I peeked through the glass window of the oven to check on the crust. It was turning a lovely golden color. Following the recipe's suggestion, I placed a foil tent over the bird to prevent over-browning the crust. At last, the required cooking time elapsed and I turned off the oven, allowing the bird to rest before carving.

Before our guests arrived, I put the finishing touches on our feast table. Place card turkeys I made from pinecones added some color. The table was set and iced tea poured when the doorbell rang. Our first invitees entered and commented on the wonderful aroma of the turkey as they set their food on card tables, our makeshift buffet. Finally, all were gathered, and my husband said grace. He helped me take the turkey out of the oven and place it on a serving platter before slicing into it.

As the bird was carved, I was immensely thankful all turned out well. The meal, a delicious success, satisfied everyone. All guests took extra turkey home with them as they left.

My maiden voyage as a "Turkey in Crust" cook gave me confidence to tackle even more complicated dishes in the future. But that first turkey, baked on my own, remains the one I remember with great fondness.

ERIKA GILES

White-Tailed Turkey

HAVING A DEEP-FRIED TURKEY for Thanksgiving dinner sounded like a great idea. My husband Leon's younger brother Dennis, who would be joining us in Seattle from Boise, had offered to prepare it. All I needed to do was make the accompaniments—mashed potatoes, yams, sage dressing, green beans, and a relish tray. I welcomed the idea of sleeping in on the holiday for a change; of not wrestling with a raw, clammy turkey while still in my bathrobe; of spending only half the day in the kitchen. And we would have a moist, tasty bird in a fraction of the time that it would take to roast one. Dennis had perfected the process of injecting a turkey with marinade and frying it in boiling oil over several years of summer family gatherings. We were all fans. This time, rather than hauling his own equipment, he planned to buy a rig in Seattle and leave it with his son, Colin, an accomplished cook, to enable him to follow in his father's deep-frying footsteps.

I admit, I *did* have misgivings about the two of them invading my kitchen with a raw turkey while I cooked the rest of the meal. Decades earlier, when Leon and I were first married, I had inadvertently left

---

Erika Giles has completed certificate programs in fiction and non-fiction writing at the University of Washington. Her essays have appeared in The Seattle Times *and other Puget Sound area publications,* Clackamas Literary Review, North Dakota Quarterly, *and* Ascent. *She lives with her husband on Mercer Island, Washington.*

a thawed turkey out on the kitchen counter overnight. A friend far more experienced with turkeys than I advised me to go ahead and roast it anyway and I did—fortunately with no ill effects. But that close call made me zealous about avoiding salmonella poisoning. Would Dennis and Colin adhere to my stringent anti-cross-contamination standards? "Don't worry," Leon assured me, a trace of amusement in his green eyes at the futility of making such a suggestion to a chronic worrier. "They'll prepare the bird for frying at Colin's apartment, and bring everything they need with them."

Dennis and Colin arrived at 1:00 on Thanksgiving afternoon, the marinated, foil-wrapped turkey in tow. Clad in jeans and sweatshirts, they seemed well-prepared for the task at hand. I was slicing celery and chopping onions for the dressing, to ensure that my part of the meal was ready when the turkey was done a couple of hours later. Dennis plopped the bird down on the tile counter. After greetings and some family chit-chat, he turned to me.

"Do you have any oil?" he asked, holding up the half-filled jug they had brought.

"Just this," I said, pulling a small bottle of olive oil from the cupboard.

"We'll need a lot more than that," Dennis said, stroking the dark stubble on his chin as Colin, taller and huskier than his father, looked on.

I refrained from pointing out to my lovable curmudgeon of a brother-in-law that I'd been told they were bringing their own supplies. "Good thing QFC stayed open this year," I told him instead. The three men piled into Dennis's Jeep Cherokee and drove to the nearby grocery store. Soon they were back, toting three jugs of Crisco oil.

I scrubbed potatoes and yams and sliced them. The guys hauled the oversized pot, heating element, stand, and propane tank from Dennis's car, through the garage, and out the back door of our suburban rambler. Glancing outside, I noticed that they were setting up on the patio.

"Not there," I called through the screen door. "Oil might splatter on the concrete." I wasn't willing to sacrifice our bluestone-lined patio, even for fried turkey.

"Oh, right," Leon said. Caught up in his relatives' enthusiasm, he hadn't considered the project's potential to inflict serious damage. He helped Dennis and Colin move the rig farther back, onto the grass. Just as they set it in place, it started to rain—not just a drop here and there, but a typical, late-November Seattle deluge. Leon ran to the storage shed to retrieve our patio umbrella and opened it over the impromptu outdoor cookery. He and his companions propped it against a tree branch and jammed sticks into the ground near its base. It held, but leaned at a rakish angle. Dennis poured oil in the pot and turned up the heat.

"Too bad about the rain," I said, when the soggy trio returned to the house.

"No problem," my ever-optimistic spouse replied, giving me a peck on the cheek before they retreated to the den to watch football.

A half-hour later, Dennis went outside to check the oil. "It's boiling," he announced. Pulling the turkey from the refrigerator, he carried it outside, his helpers trailing him. They attached a pole to the turkey's hind end and gingerly lowered it neck-first into the cauldron.

Soon they were back. So was the turkey, now slick with oil. "We have a problem," Dennis said. The turkey was longer than the oil was deep. Its front end was fully immersed; its rear parts stuck out like an iceberg floating in the ocean.

"Now what?" I asked.

"We'll need to add more oil," Dennis said. But doing that would cool the oil already in the pot and delay the time that the turkey could start cooking.

"I'll slow things down," I said. Dennis figured he could have the turkey ready by 4:00, an hour later than we had planned to eat. He and Colin went out to add the extra oil. "I could have had the whole dinner ready by now," I hissed to Leon.

"But it wouldn't have been half as much fun," he replied with a mischievous grin. He and his relatives apparently enjoyed dodging raindrops, huddling under the patio umbrella, manipulating the turkey into and out of boiling oil. A true male-bonding ritual.

When the oil was again boiling, the guys lowered the turkey into it. As they trooped back into the house, their faces were glum. "The tail is still sticking out," Dennis reported. "But we'll have to go with it." The pot was filled to capacity.

Dennis's younger son, Avery, and his girlfriend, Nikki, arrived, laden with pumpkin and pecan pies. "When do we eat?" Avery asked, looking around the kitchen. "I'm starving."

"Later than you think," I said. While Dennis regaled them with the turkey misadventures of the last couple of hours, I put out cheese and crackers to tide us over until dinner.

At 4:00, my part of the meal was ready to serve. But it was only then that the turkey finished frying. Dennis and Colin pulled it out of the pot and brought it into the house on a cutting board. The bird looked magnificent, its crispy skin a rich golden brown—until you looked at the tail. Two inches of raw, white flesh. I kept the rest of the meal warm while the turkey cooled and Dennis carved it, leaving a generous margin of cooked meat around that offending extremity. At 4:30, our fractious fowl—minus its pale tail—was finally ready to eat. My overheated mashed potatoes were disintegrating and my green beans were mushy. As always, the turkey was juicy and delicious. Still, a question hung over our Thanksgiving feast. Had salmonella migrated from the uncooked tail to the breast and drumsticks we were consuming with such gusto? We didn't know. But either it hadn't, or luck was finally with us. No one got sick.

A couple of years later, Dennis again came for Thanksgiving, but I decided not to take any chances. I roasted a turkey.

FAWN HAHNENBERG

Shanghai'd Thanksgiving

IT HAD BEEN just three months since we boarded a plane bound for China, and transitioning to life in Shanghai was going much smoother than anticipated. It wasn't until confronted with the impending arrival of Thanksgiving, a truly traditional, American holiday, I realized just how far from home we truly were.

For me, Thanksgiving meant spending the day with family, eating and eating and eating until it became imperative to change into pants with an elastic waistband, while enjoying the closeness that being with family brings. I was determined to recreate that tradition with my own children, and in order to accomplish this, I first needed to find a turkey. Without a turkey, Thanksgiving might as well be on a Tuesday in July. It cannot be celebrated without a turkey. Period.

In November in the United States, turkey is not only plentiful but cheap. Many stores offer promotions, and if taken advantage of, the turkey is easily the least expensive item on the menu—not so in China. Turkey, being indigenous to North and South America, are neither wild nor farmed in any part of Asia. And although there are 19 million people in Shanghai, only a select group of expatriates want to eat them... and only once a year. Therefore, the average 15-pound gobbler will set you back approximately $100 U.S. dollars.

Fawn Hahnenberg is a stay-at-home mom and writer with an inability to cook a decent turkey. When not living in Shanghai, China, with her husband and two boys, ages five and nine, she calls Michigan home.

In addition to the requisite turkey, the menu also included mashed potatoes and gravy, rolls, corn, fresh vegetables with dip, and Jell-O. Despite the simplicity of the ingredients, finding them required scouring five different stores over three days and cost a small fortune. But I did it! I found everything I needed, including the myriad of spices to make brine, which was sure to be the one thing that brought the simple bill of fare to five-star restaurant status.

Thanksgiving Day, after consulting with both Betty Crocker and Butterball.com, I determined the bird would take approximately four hours to cook at a temperature of about 350 degrees. I carefully converted Fahrenheit to Centigrade and decided to set the oven at 170 degrees.

While the oven was warming, my husband pulled the bird from the brine, which had been soaking up the lovely, savory flavors overnight, only to discover the pan I'd purchased was too small. It was like trying to squeeze a size ten foot into a strappy, little size seven shoe. It just wasn't going to work.

In my shopping excursions that week, I noticed some of the stores stocked with disposable pans. I crossed my fingers as I ran on foot to the closest little market. I was in luck. Covered in dust and tucked away on a back shelf, they had just one. I snatched it up and ran home.

We were now ready to throw the main course into the gas chamber, but the new pan was too big for the tiny oven. After performing a little origami fused with some karate chops on the cheap aluminum, the pan fit.

With the turkey safely roasting, I took the kids to the park for the afternoon. When I returned, I started peeling the potatoes. By my estimation, the bird would be done in 30 minutes. I opened the oven door to check its progress. NO FLAME. At some point during the day, the gas had blown out and while the temperature in the oven dropped, the tension in the kitchen soared.

We had no idea how long the turkey had not been roasting, and this particular bird had no plastic indicator to let us know when it was time to carve, so we did the next best thing and stuck a thermometer in it. My husband punctured the breast and watched while the temperature gauge rose.

"According to Betty, the thermometer is supposed to go in the thigh," I informed him after consulting the red and white-checkered cookbook.

"Where's the thigh?" he replied.

"I'm not exactly sure," I said, "but I know that's not it."

He left the thermometer in the breast and we watched as it climbed to 130 degrees Fahrenheit. The kids were starting to moan and groan and whine. They were "staaaarving." So I presented them with veggies and dip and we started to snack while we waited another estimated hour for the bird to reach a safe temperature to eat.

When the thermometer started to beep, indicating the turkey had reached temperature, I began to set the table. While my husband whipped the mashed potatoes into creamy goodness and heated the corn, he snuck a bite of a dinner roll... and then promptly spit it out. The rolls were filled with sweet cream and raisins. We'd spent several hours the day before going from one bakery to the next in search of anything that resembled a dinner roll. The little surprise inside of these was unexpected and unappreciated. I remembered seeing a French baguette at the store earlier, so I put on my running shoes and sprinted there a second time. Again, I felt very lucky. No one else had purchased the single loaf of bread on the shelf. I paid for it and raced back home.

Finally, we were ready to eat. The table was set, the candles were lit, and we said our prayers of thanksgiving. Just as we were about to carve the turkey, in the flicker of the candlelight, I noticed a lot of juice on the platter. I jumped out of my seat and threw on the lights.... BLOOD! The entire ambience was ruined as the bird was not even close to being edible. Frustrated, my husband cut the gobbler wide open and put it back in the oven at 400 degrees Fahrenheit. He sliced off a large piece of breast meat, nuked it, and sat down to eat. I fed the kids Jell-O while I waited for the turkey to finish roasting. At 8 P.M., I opened the oven door to check on the bird. NO FLAME!

After eight hours of failed attempts to roast the perfect turkey, I surrendered. I put everything away, did the dishes, and bathed the kids. Once they were safely tucked into bed, I broke out the Pop Tarts. Happy Thanksgiving to me!

Epilogue:

We just celebrated our third and best Thanksgiving yet while living in China. There was not a turkey anywhere near the premises, just great friends and lots of laughs. I was wrong. While eating turkey is a nice addition to the holiday, it is ultimately *who* you spend the day with that matters most—not what's on the menu.

LEON CONTAVESPRIE

Thank You for the Music

BEING A STUDENT, I have learned to look forward to the holidays not just because I get to go home and see my family, but also because I can get away from the not-so-stimulating world of academia. Needless to say, with Thanksgiving coming up, I am getting a little giddy. My step is a little quicker, my disposition a little brighter, and I am all around a much nicer person than I was, say, two weeks ago.

That said, I was walking towards the aptly named Payne Center (our fitness facility on the Southern Miss campus) to catch my usual Saturday morning workout, when a large black wall caught my eye. I saw that it was the Vietnam Memorial Moving Wall (forgive me if that's not the official title). Since I have heard about this monument but have never seen it, I decided to walk over and pay a visit.

I now know why it is called the "Moving Wall." The tears rolled down my face as I read what seemed like thousands of names of fallen soldiers, most of whom were younger than I am now. I turned around to walk away when I collided into a middle-aged man wearing a POW-MIA shirt. I pardoned myself and proceeded down the walk, but my curiosity got the best of me, so I turned back to him

---

Leon Contavesprie is a native of New Orleans, and received an MFA in Performance from the University of Southern Mississippi in 2003.

and asked, "Excuse me, but do you know anyone on the wall?" He said, "Yes... my brother."

I guess the stunned look on my face spoke volumes because he added, "Would you like to see his name?" I thought about it for just a second, kind of afraid of what was coming next, but finally I said, "Yes, I would."

We walked about 25 feet; he hunkered down and pointed to a name near the bottom of the wall. "How old was he?" I asked. After a few seconds, he replied, "19."

His age alone caught me off guard. All I could think to say was, "You must be very proud."

"Young man," he said, "You have no idea. You see, he was five years older than me and I worshipped the ground he walked on." The smile on his face grew as he went on. "He used to play the clarinet and God how I loved to listen when he practiced. He was so good—I'd watch him for hours. The sound seemed to come from his soul. He had just started teaching me to play when he was drafted. When he was gone and I'd get scared, I'd remember his music and I'd feel safe. I'll never forget that. The sad thing is I never got to thank him for it."

He then shook my hand. "Thanks for remembering with me," he said. The man whose first name I'll never know walked quietly away. I stood there almost comatose for a few minutes, not really knowing how I felt.

I do know this, though—Thanksgiving means a lot more to me than it did two weeks ago. The man who I will probably never see again taught me more in that one minute than I've learned in 16 years of school. His lesson was so simple; it's amazing how I had never realized it before. Millions of us are blessed with family and friends, who give so much of themselves every day, but we often take them and what they do for granted. So, to anyone who has graciously added a special melody to my heart, I sincerely say thank you for the music.

HOLLY RUTCHIK

Turkey, Shoes and Tights

IT WAS THANKSGIVING and the first time she had ever worn tights. I watched her kick her black, knit-covered legs in her new, big-girl car seat. She sucked her thumb and explored her newly spacious travel accommodations. I envied her comfort. I turned back in my seat and pulled at the seatbelt as if it were to blame for my discomfort.

"If I'm this huge next Thanksgiving, I'll kill you," I threatened my husband.

"Well, I'll see what I can do," he responded, a bit of fear in his voice.

I'd been pregnant for almost two straight years. I had barked all week about how this baby had better be out by Thanksgiving. I wasn't in a thankful mood as we loaded up the car for Thanksgiving dinner with his extended family. There was still an empty infant car seat in the back, and I was still pregnant.

Strapped in the back seat was last year's holiday momento. I had been due the previous Thanksgiving Day with the "baby" who was now a toddler wearing tights. She came early last year, and by

---

Holly Rutchik is a freelance writer living in Wisconsin with her husband, Joseph, and their daughters, Tessa and Anna Clare. She holds a Master of Arts in Religious Studies and can be found blogging about faith, writing, and motherhood at fallingupwardholly.blogspot.com. She can be reached at hollyrutchik@yahoo.com.

Thanksgiving Day, I was holding my new baby, eating turkey and watching football at my family's Thanksgiving gathering.

"We didn't expect you this year!" relative after relative said as they walked through the autumn wreath-covered door, pies and crock-pots in hand.

"Well, this baby knew I couldn't miss a Thanksgiving at home!" I responded as I held my newborn daughter.

It was true; I'd never missed a Thanksgiving at home. When "I" became a "we," there was no flip-flopping this holiday, I always got Thanksgiving. I'm from the country and holidays celebrated in the country are the makings of postcards—picture perfect.

Now here I was, 12 months later and nine months pregnant, on my way to my first Thanksgiving away from home. I was due any minute, and the long car ride to my hometown was out of the question. I would not be eating my aunt Barb's famous corn casserole this year.

Thanksgiving is by far my favorite meal. When asked, "What's your favorite food?" My response has always been, "Thanksgiving!" In graduate school and living on little more than pipe dreams, I made what I called "poor man's Thanksgiving" on a weekly basis. Instant stuffing, potato spuds and "just add water" gravy really is nostalgically tasty.

I rolled down the window and stuck my arm out, as if trying to catch the Thanksgiving as it slipped through my fingers with the fall wind. I was stuck in a short, dramatic period of transition, similar to the Wisconsin weather in November. I was on Year Three of what was becoming a bad holiday tradition of life transitions.

I'd had a Thanksgiving weekend bridal shower, and by the time the stores were stocking their shelves with turkey and fixings the next fall, I had the little gal who now sat in the back seat, kicking her legs and enjoying her tights. (She was sans shoes, which I would hear about from my mother-in-law before the turkey was carved.)

This year, I was waiting on a baby. In the same closet where my daughter's forgotten shoes sat, a tiny pilgrim outfit hung waiting. An outfit my husband would kill me for if he knew I had purchased, especially now, since it has no owner.

Besides, I had my own shoe crisis this Thanksgiving. There is a chance my one-year-old can pull off a shoeless outfit at a family gathering, but no chance for a grown woman, no matter how pregnant.

My husband had found me that morning in the back closet, shrieking, "Oh no! Help!"

"What, What?!" he shouted.

He was expecting to find me standing in a puddle, my water broken. Instead, he found a crazed woman hurling shoe after shoe out of the closet.

"I don't have any shoes to wear, as in, I can't get any of them on my feet!" I explained frantically.

We hatched a plan for me to carry a pair of shoes to the car, put them on to walk through the front door of his aunt and uncle's house, and immediately remove them once inside. The hope that I could pass the whole thing off as being polite by removing my shoes in their home was as dim as my hope that going into labor would prevent me from having to execute the plan. I briefly considered not going, but it was Thanksgiving, after all. If I couldn't be pushing a baby out, I was going to be pushing food in!

As I sat in the car on my way to a Thanksgiving away from home, I recalled how easy instant Thanksgiving would be to make, or buy in a box sitting in the frozen foods section. I leaned my head against the cool glass of the frosted car window. November in Wisconsin smells and sounds so crisp. The smell of the air matches the soundtrack of trotting over crispy leaves whose summer life has dried up, but now lay fallen on the frosting ground. Winter teases with a slight kiss. Its frigidness stings the lungs on a full breath. This Thanksgiving, I couldn't enjoy that smell. I was too huge to take it all in with a deep breath. I wanted to snuggle with blankets on the cold bleachers of a local high school football game. Instead, I was so uncomfortable, I could barely stand being touched. I was now on my way to a family function where I'd have to hug a dozen in-laws. As fast as fall daylight hours disappear, so were my spirits with each leafless tree we drove by.

"Is she sleeping?" my husband asked.

"What?" I replied, taking a moment to come out of my pity party.

"Can you check and see if she's sleeping?" he asked.

I turned to look at my first Thanksgiving baby. Today she would have her first Thanksgiving meal. I was excited about the traditional foods I'd mash up and watch her devour while making a mess of her first holiday dress. And in that moment—as any nine-months-pregnant woman holds the right to do—I changed my mind as I watched her play in her new car seat. Instead of feeling resentful and huge, I felt thankful to have this last holiday as a family of three. One last family day before the life we knew would be turned upside-down with another blessing.

"No," I answered. "I don't think she's going to fall asleep, she's hungry," I said with a smile.

This Thanksgiving we'll celebrate our second daughter's first birthday. I won't be going into labor this year. Instead, we'll be traveling to my hometown, and giving yet another little girl her first taste of pumpkin pie. We'll enjoy an uneventful Thanksgiving in the country as a family of four. Our two little pilgrims will be wearing tights, and I'll be wearing shoes.

CHARLES CASSADY JR.

A Few Words of Contrariness from a Thanksgiving Hater

I DESPISE THANKSGIVING.

This flat statement has brought me the proverbial cornucopia of shocked reactions over the years. "How can you NOT like Thanksgiving? It's the greatest holiday there is! There's so much good stuff to eat!" . . . And so on. I could have offended fewer people by declaring that I don't like Christmas, or I don't Support the Troops, or I don't Save the Whales.

Yet I won't bring myself to embrace this pseudo-holiday that blights the calendar every November. I am Thanksgiving's equivalent of Ebeneezer Scrooge. Any three ghosts of Thanksgivings Past, Present, and Future who materialize at my door to reform me will be boiled in their own gravy and buried with a sharpened cob of maize in their hearts.

Charles Cassady Jr. is a writer and photographer near Cleveland, Ohio. He is also author of Cleveland Ghosts, Paranormal Great Lakes, *and sundry pop-culture compilations. His articles and reviews have run in the* Cleveland Free Times, Common Sense Media, TVGuide.com, *and* The Morning Journal of Lorain.

While certain fourth Thursdays in Novembers stand out as worse than others, I cannot point to one single trauma that turned me into such an overwhelming Thanksgiving Day misanthrope overnight. True, it was a Thanksgiving week that I realized that my first girlfriend didn't especially love me, or even particularly like me. True, I was an infant in my crib during the Thanksgiving week in 1963 when President John F. Kennedy was assassinated, followed by the shooting of accused assassin Lee Harvey Oswald. Maybe a nation's collective psychic agony somehow imprinted itself into my developing consciousness.

Or, perhaps the die was cast just because I was born the same wounded month, November. Thus my birthday and Thanksgiving became fatefully intertwined in my mind—the dates doing their little dance around each other. As I get older and become more of a curmudgeon, my birthdays become less and less desirable observances. Thanksgiving may have been caught up, through no fault of its own, in my general orneriness. How dare everyone be so happy when I'm one year older and more miserable. If only my hatred of Thanksgiving began and ended with that. Then the fault would be mine and mine alone.

But there is more. Even from early childhood—back when I still indeed enjoyed my birthdays—I fostered a sneaking suspicion that something was just wrong about this "Thanksgiving," a holiday that no other nation on Earth seemed to share. If the coincident birthday was heredity, then environment also made its baleful contribution to the growing unease—an accumulation of negatives that ultimately boiled over like a fire-hazard turkey roaster.

I grew up in the midst of the Great Lakes rust belt, in an industrial town which, ever since I could read newspapers and comprehend the evening news, seemed on an economic downward spiral. With every passing month, more layoffs, more department downsizing and streamlining, more recession, more companies either pulling up stakes and getting out of Dodge (well, Cleveland, to be precise) or failing completely.

Soon I came to know the concept of "fourth-quarter earnings" in big business. Meaning that unseen drones in cubicles waited until November to announce how many workers to let go, how many livelihoods to wreck, as the end of the year approached, to make the company books balance, to please the shareholders to earn their generous hatchet-men bonuses. It always struck me as perverse that a Thanksgiving holiday, supposed to be a time to pause and reflect on a bountiful harvest and man's generosity to man, came heralded by corporate hit-lists methodically terminating thousands and thousands of job-holders.

Was I ever one of those job-holders? Is that the reason for my sour applesauce, you might ask?

No, I was never even that lucky to have a job to lose in the first place. In my foolish youth, for reasons that seemed (sigh) Like A Good Idea At The Time, the prospect of a career in writing-communications looked especially suitable. I compounded that mistake exponentially, by attending a costly, out-of-state college to obtain my Journalism degree (and indeed, having to traverse a couple of wintry states going back home for every Thanksgiving Break disrupted my diligent studies for finals and added to my annoyance over the inconvenient holiday).

Graduation from this institution was a festive and delirious affair—Governor Mario Cuomo of New York officiated as our A-list Commencement speaker. Little did I suspect that it marked the commencement, indeed, of a three-decade dry spell during which I would be almost continuously unemployed. Know that I come from a successful family. I do not at all begrudge them the prosperity that rose from their hard work; they earned every dime of it, and I am glad my relatives put up with me to any extent. Still, I ask you to imagine my discomfort every Thanksgiving, as we gathered in the hearth-fire warmth of one of my rich uncles' yacht clubs (it sounds like a cliché, but I assure you, quite true).

There around the feasting-table, I would hear each relation in turn discuss their windfalls from valuable stock-splits, booming investments, the ascending Dow Jones average. And if conversation ever turned to me and how I was doing? Well, I would have to stutter, the ad agency that was going to pay me $50 per month for freelancing backed out of the deal. And that small-time entertainment mag in Syracuse that was talking about sending me to do an interview with Molly Ringwald? Out of business. Oh, but wire services might engage me as a photo stringer—at $25 per assignment. All I had to do was provide my own $2,500 pro photo gear. Good thing I still lived in my parents' place and could start saving up.

Happy Thanksgiving, yes indeedy. My resentment ran over the dishes like cranberry sauce.

College did provide me with one important insight, however. As I bent, fascinated, over copies of old newspapers and historical journals in the campus library, I had an epiphany about the historical origins of Thanksgiving. It goes far back in the dusty vaults of time, to a period when a much younger American continent was trodden by caravans of ill-clothed, ill-provisioned, smelly and often disease-plagued adventurers. Men and women journeying far outside their accustomed clime in search of a better life. These ragged pioneers of olden days, these forefathers, these ancestors... we now call "hippies."

Yes, I blame the Age-of-Aquarius counterculture for the well-ingrained veneration of Thanksgiving, of this one holiday enduring in a time of fallen idols and blasted dreams. It was the university-based youth-in-rebellion movement of the 1960s—the ones who burned draft cards, bras, American flags, and tubfuls of marijuana—the ones who promised Revolution but mainly succeeded in being revolting, who made Thanksgiving their very own, the lone sacrosanct calendar holiday. As I interpret it, Thanksgiving provided these underaged leftist hooligans with a nice, non-religious (none of their parents' squaresville God stuff that they didn't dig) reason to convene at their local Alice's Restaurant, to embrace one another in celebratory comradeship. To make merry. To feast on the fruits of the earth. To smoke some joints and set aside for a moment the pressing ideological quandaries about whether to bomb the ROTC building next or set fire to the faculty offices first (or just smoke more dope).

The hippies may have all since joined the mainstream, grown gray and flabby, attained full professorships at liberal-arts universities such as the one that fleeced me, and made a tax-write-off killing by donating all their autographed Grateful Dead relics to museums (all the while, still smoking plenty of dope). But their legacy remains. Thanksgiving was enthusiastically upheld by the "freaks" as well as the "straights." And it continues to be so.

What, you may ask, of the traditional storybook-Thanksgiving tale? You know, Plymouth Rock, all that greeting-card stuff? Don't I at least find that adorable?

It makes a good story, indeed, that compassionate Indians helped rescue and succor the starving Mayflower arrivals. In fact, I would ask all of you Thanksgiving-fanciers to go right to your neighborhood tribal Longhouse and thank the chief personally. Oh wait a minute, that's right. There is no neighborhood tribal Longhouse. There is no chief. The Indians, the original Americans, were, for all practical purposes, genocidally wiped off the map by artillery, smallpox, and the white man's firewater. Their sacred sites were desecrated, turned into strip malls. How silly of me to forget. Must be all this nice roast beef.

It's not as though I wish the original Plymouth colony had been massacred by the Indians. Nothing so extreme. The red men, recognizing the threat these starving palefaces posed, should just have invaded, taken everyone hostage, forced them to adopt Indian ways, learn to make guns of their own. The Indians could then have formed a veritable Homeland Security of defensive alliances with all the other tribes, their lookouts, and cannon arrayed along the eastern seaboard for any future scurvy European landings. Maybe strategic harbors would have been marked with big signs facing out to the ocean reading, "BEWARE: DANGEROUS SASQUATCHES. SAVE YOURSELVES AND TURN YOUR SHIPS AROUND."

Curiously, I've learned, before the great white brothers arrived, certain American Indians had a Thanksgiving-like celebration of their own. Osage legends tell of an ancient "Battle of the Monsters," in which giant, hairy, horned animals invaded from the east, crossing over the Mississippi. The native animals of the Missouri territory, outraged at the intrusion, fought with the monsters, leaving many dead on both sides. What monsters from the east survived the clash, fled westward out of the region, and the Osage ancestors burned the huge carcasses of the fallen as a sacrifice to the Great Spirit for their deliverance. An annual ritual of thanks over the Battle of the Monsters, held at a distinct, table-shaped rock formation on Big Bone River, became an Osage tradition. After the Louisiana Purchase, the tale, in parable form, was indeed used to rally Osage braves in the battle of yet another intruder from the east, the white man. I think we all know how that fight went. In an epilogue, an Army Corps of Engineers dam project would end up submerging most of the sacred sites associated with this truly Indian "thanksgiving."

Don't ask me for footnotes and citations for the following. I read it somewhere of late, and whether vicious anti-American propaganda or gospel truth about the dark side of the "winning of the west," it dovetails with my opinion of Thanksgiving. It seems that early on, after President George Washington instituted the thing as the first U.S. holiday by presidential proclamation, certain communities on the wild frontier had a clever idea. They would throw "Thanksgiving" banquets and invite the nearest Indians. When the Indians arrived, the friendly settlers would open fire and kill them, all in a single stroke. Via such systematic murder, the happy homesteaders would acquire more land and, one presumes, more reasons to give thanks to Almighty God for the largesse.

Nice holiday you've got there, folks.

And now for dessert, if you will. My final reason for hating Thanksgiving.

One of my vivid earliest memories is petting an especially docile turkey at a farm. I'd probably met other domesticated animals, but probably never a bird that was so patient and quiet while I stroked its wrinkly head and called it "my best friend." Doubtlessly, this gentle farm turkey was straightway slaughtered and served up for food. I do not loudly bang the drum for animal rights—I just try to eat as little meat as possible (actually pretty easy when you're a struggling writer; you can't afford it anyway) and hope that my own modest lifestyle does not introduce a greater burden of undue cruelty into the world. But other activists and writers are not being so timid, the latest being best-selling novelist Jonathan Safran Foer. They have scrutinized the factory-farm industry and used their considerable literary talents to describe the horror of those assembly-lines that spew out grotesquely growth-hormoned beef and poultry products for Thanksgiving tables every November. I'll spare the hideous details... and just ask those of you who insist on gorging yourselves to look into the "turkey-free Thanksgiving" movements, such as the one created by the

Vegetarian Awareness Network, that try to promote meat substitutes. Do it in memory of my onetime best friend.

As I said, I do not bang the drum for animal rights. I do not join those types who don animal costumes (probably made out of genuine polar bear and Siberian tiger fur) and march around, disrupting traffic. But I can too-easily put myself in the position of feeling very much like a caged bird in a labyrinth of a giant agri-business factory, bewildered and helpless, on a conveyor belt, with knives waiting at the end...

Or I can feel like a vulnerable employee as the fourth-quarter-earnings period looms—all too aware that my job hangs by a thread, and an axe awaits me in the end, as the customary office decorations of autumn leaves and cartoon pilgrims with blunderbusses remind me what time of year it is...

Or I can feel like a trepidatious Indian, invited by the invading white settlers to something they call "Thanksgiving," seeing the sun glint off their steel in the distance as I draw closer...

Down with Thanksgiving, I say!

D. M. WILMES

Our Last Thanksgiving with Mom

THANKSGIVING was just two weeks away. Mom and Dad had planned on hosting the holiday at their house for all 30-plus people, like they did every year since I could remember. It was a much-anticipated family tradition, and, each year, Mom went all out for the event by setting out her best dinnerware and preparing nearly every culinary delight from scratch. It was evident by this time that she would not be able to cater such a large affair. Her health had deteriorated to the point that it was difficult for her to move around on her own. Dad asked if we could hold it at our house. We gladly obliged. My wife, Patti, and I set out to rearrange our house to accommodate the large gathering. As Thanksgiving approached, I took days off work to help prepare the feast. Patti and I looked forward to having everyone over, and we wanted to make this Thanksgiving extra special for Mom and Dad.

We joined two long tables together to form one massive, contiguous slab that stretched from the kitchen into our adjoining living room. We set out our best china dishes, silverware, and glassware.

D. M. Wilmes is a Missouri writer who has worked in the IT industry for over 20 years. He proudly supports Susan G. Komen for the Cure and its efforts to save lives and end breast cancer forever. www.dmwilmes.com

Chilled wine, pumpkin bread, cranberries, and customary condiments were placed at frequent intervals to limit the passing of food from one end of the room to the other. No detail was left unanswered. It was just as Mom would have done.

On the eve of Thanksgiving, Patti and I heated the large roasting ovens borrowed a week before from Dad. They were now brimming with pulled turkey and Mom's special raisin bread dressing that I had attempted to do her proud by duplicating. As we readied the house for the holiday affair, the phone rang. It was Dad. He broke the news to us that they would probably not be able to make it. Mom had become considerably weaker, and Dad was deeply concerned because her slurring had worsened. He asked us to continue with the holiday feast for the rest of the family. If she was able, they would come, but the probability was low. I tried to query Dad for answers, but he kept his voice low and only answered with brief and awkward replies. Once I realized he was intentionally shielding his conversation, as well as his concern, from Mom, I grudgingly tapered my inquiry.

Mom had batlike senses. Perhaps it came from raising six children. It was difficult to sneak anything past her. In any case, Dad wasn't able to speak freely to me, and I understood. After we hung up, my heart sank. It wouldn't be the same without them. It angered me that the doctors could find nothing when it was apparent something was obviously wrong. It would be a melancholy Thanksgiving at best, and I wanted to cancel it. How could any of us celebrate the holiday without them? Per Dad's wishes, however, we reluctantly went on with our plans.

By early afternoon of Thanksgiving, family members began to arrive, all bearing homemade side dishes, desserts, and spirits. Soon, brothers, sisters, spouses, and children bustled about the house. Wine bottles were uncorked, while warming trays dispensed aromas of sweet potatoes and casseroles. The walls echoed the rumors of Mom's latest condition, and it was all we could talk about. It dampened the normally festive occasion and the tone was subdued. Mom and Dad were always the nucleus of any family get-together, and it seemed disrespectful to be celebrating the holiday without them.

Just when we thought all had arrived who would arrive, the doorbell rang. It was Dad at our doorstep. Mom was clutching his arm.

"You made it!" I exclaimed while opening the door.

Others heard the announcement and rushed to the entryway. What I saw next nearly brought tears to my eyes. Dad led his beloved wife into the corridor. She could barely walk on her own and shuffled across the tile floor.

"I made it," she said with a smile. Her words were so slurred, I could hardly understand her. It was as if she were drunk on holiday wine.

I hugged her and welcomed her. I could tell it pained her to return the gesture. Every movement was slow and labored. It was as though she had aged 40 years since I'd seen her only a few days ago. She even made light of her speech.

"I must have started drinking without you," she joked.

I wanted to crawl into a hole and cry. Whatever was afflicting her had reduced her to a shell of an old woman who could barely walk, much less speak. We were all aghast, but we hid it the best we could with love and affection.

We tried to carry on as usual on that Thanksgiving Day, drinking wine, overindulging on pecan and pumpkin pie, telling stories of the past, laughing and joking, but Mom's condition weighed heavily on all of us. Dad, who had quit smoking years ago, had started again. Those of us who smoked, and even those who didn't, met with him on the deck each time he had a cigarette. He tried to keep his smoking from Mom, although she knew what he was doing and rarely said anything. He was so upset. Several times he cried. He was lost and, like us, wanted to know what was wrong.

At one point, Dad gathered all of us children on the deck and explained that doctors would perform a brain scan the following day. Once again, they would be looking for cancer, although nerve damage was another possible culprit. As much as we tried to cling to the latter prognosis, Dad stressed several times that nerve damage was a very remote possibility. He negated it as though he had already been informed of the results from the pending test. Dad was astute at reading people and understanding what is conveyed between the lines. He must have picked up on something the doctor had said, as he never seriously considered the possibility of nerve damage.

Later in the afternoon, Mom mentioned the same thing. Her outlook was always positive, and she had a sense of humor. "They're going to do a brain scan," she said. Apparently we didn't disguise our concerned expressions very well. "Oh, don't worry. I'm sure it's just nerve damage or something. I think they just want to see if there really is a brain up there."

She said she felt fine, other than just being tired all of the time and unable to speak clearly. To her, it didn't have the familiar signature of cancer she had desperately battled the year before.

Already aware of Dad's version, we supported her in her theory and never let on we were informed otherwise. That was one of the hardest things I've ever had to do. Mom knew they were looking for cancer again, but I wasn't sure if she was protecting us or honestly held hope that it was something less destructive. Whatever her reasoning, the word cancer never escaped her lips.

By late afternoon, Mom was tiring and asked to go home. We wanted her to stay longer, but our persuasions were not enough to overcome her fatigue. Dad dutifully fetched Mom's coat from the hall closet, carefully lifted her from her chair, and wrapped her coat around her shoulders. She didn't have the strength to lift her arms into the sleeves. We bid our extended farewells, indulging in as many hugs as slices of pie we had eaten that day, as Dad escorted his frail wife out of our house and into the car. It was heart-wrenching to watch her leave in such a fragile condition.

Two weeks later, she passed away from an aggressive brain cancer. It was the last Thanksgiving I would spend with my mother.

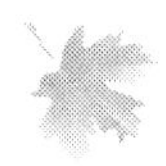

L. K. HILL

Hill vs. Hill vs. Hill

"HEY, WATCH OUT," I call, wiggling my index finger in the general direction of the disaster that's about to happen. From across a football field-sized space, however, I have little hope of being heard. As I watch, my 13-year-old brother, Tim, is thrown up against the chain-link fence that encloses the field and then smashed into it by his two older brothers, one of which weighs more than 200 pounds.

I run the width of the field to make sure he's all right. By the time I get there, he is laying on his back, facing the sky, body limp and limbs lifeless. It reminds me of the Far Side joke about the boneless chicken farm. I would be worried except that he is laughing hysterically. Despite being pancaked into a chain-link fence—and having the grid marks all over his right cheek to prove it—he's managed to hold on to the football. When he finds the strength to stand, he holds it over his head victoriously and his team—consisting of our entire immediate family—cheers.

My uncle and cousins, who make up the other team, are muttering variations of "Aw, man!" and "Chump," under their breaths, though not very quietly.

L. K. Hill is a graduate of Weber State University and is currently living and working in Ogden, Utah. She is a working writer and aspiring novelist. She comes from a close-knit family of fourteen.

It's the annual Hill vs. Hill Thanksgiving football game. A large, fenced field almost directly next door to my parents' house is the stage for the extravagant game. Our family of 12 kids and my Uncle Bryson's family of nine—seven children—grew up together. Needless to say, our family get-togethers can be quite the circus.

On the next pass, my brother, Nick, throws a pass my way. It's impeccable. He throws it with dead-on accuracy, and I'm in the perfect spot to catch it. I don't pretend to be the world's greatest athlete, but I certainly know how to catch a football. I would have, too... if my cousin's fiancée—who is two feet taller than I am—hadn't come out of nowhere, lifted his arms slightly to reach a height I can't touch jumping, and plucked the football nonchalantly from the air.

And suddenly, I'm the bad guy!

"Oh come on, Liesel, jump for those!"

"Aw, man! Why'd you let him get the interception?"

"Someone needs to grow some longer arms..."

"Hey," I holler, "it's not my fault I'm vertically challenged. It's Mom's fault. And Grandpa Conger's!"

No one's listening anymore, so I shrug and take my place for defense.

Nick, great quarterback though he is, was perhaps my parents'—and by extension, our family's—greatest trial. He dropped out of school in junior high and put my parents through several hellish years of bad choices, cops, courts, runaway lists, frustration, and heartache. My parents never stopped loving him, but they had to let him go, and let him learn the hard lessons of life on his own. He was picked up on light drug charges and petty theft, and spent several years in and out of juvie.

What he saw and experienced there scared him enough to finally start getting his life together. He was now living with his girlfriend and several other disreputable persons, but he had a steady job, had gotten himself and his girlfriend clean, and was expecting a baby—my parents' first grandchild—by her.

Despite the worry, heartache, and occasional resentment we all felt while he was doing his teenaged rebellion thing, we were all so glad to see him finally on a path of progression, rather than regression, that the previous feelings and experiences were all but forgotten.

The last five years or so have been hard on the entire family. We've had our fair share of trials, as every family does. Financial difficulties plagued everyone, with the economy in ruin, and then there were the run-of-the-mill broken hearts, car accidents, and other dramas that plague everyday life.

This year, for the first time in a long while, things are looking up. Everyone is finally comfortable with their living situation, my brother is finally starting to turn his life around, everyone seems to be making ends meet, and even the economy is improving.

Even if there were still a lot of drama, though, it wouldn't matter. Our annual football game is a time when we can all kick back, have some fun, and leave the world behind us.

When we get the ball again—it doesn't take long as they score in embarrassingly record time—we all huddle up to discuss the play.

"Nice cuddle...I mean huddle," my teenaged cousins yell. We ignore them.

"Everyone understand what they're going to do?" My dad is asking.

"So," 11-year-old Bob says, "I'm just going to go up through there, right?" As he asks, he turns and points his finger, showing the other team exactly what our play was going to be.

My dad rolls his eyes and begins reworking the play while my uncle falls into a fit of hyena hysterics 20 feet away.

In the years following, Bob will get into trouble at school a lot. Nothing out of the way of normal teenaged brain damage and rebellion, but he, along with his older brother Tim, will have his turn putting his family through the ringer. The incident that took the cake was when the two of them snuck out of the house, stole my dad's car, and went joy riding at three o'clock in the morning. The cops brought them home.

Now, however, they laugh and wrestle and horseplay around with their brothers and cousins, without a care in the world.

When we girl cousins get tired of the boys hogging the ball, we sometimes just walk up and down the field, talking and visiting and catching up. Despite growing up together and being close when we were little, we are all adults now and have our own lives and friends.

Consequently, we rarely see each other except at family holidays and reunions.

My sister, McKensie, and her husband, Roy, have driven from Vegas for the day. McKensie was the first to get married, which made her the guinea pig. It took the entire family, especially the brothers, quite a while to accept Roy into the clan. Even now it's a work in progress, but progressing we are.

My sister, Tina, and I room together at college, and neither of us have ever been the rebellious type. However, we're both over 25 and unmarried, to my mother's everlasting shame. Today, though, we visit with our sisters and cousins.

When the game is finished—they win, but *we'll* never admit that—we all head toward the house. My Grandma Adams is waiting on the porch with her wide, warm eyes, easy smile, and big teddy bear hugs.

During dinner, dessert, and afterward, there will be lively conversation—dominated by my two loud-mouthed brothers, who really should have been entertainers rather than salesmen—the same old jokes and reminiscences told, and a great deal of fun.

The year before, David, the oldest boy, almost made a disastrous marriage—like Jane Austen disastrous—but was saved in the nick of time. Now, happily, he's married to a charming girl that the entire family is in love with.

For us, Thanksgiving has never been about food, though that is a happy bonus. It's never been about pilgrims or Indians or turkey. We sometimes go around in a circle and say what we're thankful for, but even that is a secondary concern.

For us, Thanksgiving is about family. It's about catching up and always knowing the people who are the most important. It's about knowing that we have a strong, permanent, trustworthy, foolproof security system in our family that will never fail us. No matter what drama is going on in our lives, it's never brought to the Thanksgiving table. My memories of Thanksgiving will always be warm, funny, unbelievably full, and happy.

DOROTHY LEYENDECKER

A Texas Thanksgiving Day

"IT'S PROBABLY my brother Chuck calling from California to wish us a Happy Thanksgiving," I called to my husband as I got out of my recliner to answer the phone in the kitchen. I had put the turkey in the oven about an hour before and had finished setting the table. Now I could have a few minutes' rest before my son Bob would arrive from Austin to spend the day with us. His wife and daughters were in Pennsylvania spending the holiday with her family while a last-minute change in his work schedule kept Bob at home.

"Hi Chuck and Karen, Happy Thanksgiving to you, too," I replied when I answered the phone. Suddenly, out of the corner of my eye, I saw what looked like a flash of white lightening. "Dick!" I shouted as I dropped the phone and ran to the oven. "The turkey is on fire."

Through the oven window, I could see what looked like lightning streaks spitting and sputtering across the bottom of the oven. Zzzzt! Zzzzt! The sounds of electricity gone amok could be heard through

---

Dorothy Leyendecker has had stories published in Reminisce *and* Good Old Days *magazines and several anthologies, including the Barnes and Noble Anthologies,* The Noble Generation Volumes II *and* III. *Her poems have appeared in various publications. She is retired in Florida and is a member of the Florida Writers Association.*

the oven door. (As I look back now, it kind of reminded me of the scene in the old Frankenstein movie when all the lab apparatus was set into motion by the lightning zig-zagging its way from one device to another.)

I turned the oven off. All was quiet. I held my breath as Dick opened the oven door. The turkey was unharmed. He showed me where the bottom heating element had broken in half, causing the short circuit.

Meanwhile, I had forgotten about the phone call. "Dorothy, Dick, what's going on there? Are you ok?" I could hear the voices coming from the floor where I had dropped the phone. After assuring my brother that we were fine, I explained what happened. We wished each other a Happy Thanksgiving and promised to get in touch soon.

We now had a half-baked turkey and a malfunctioning oven. After putting their heads together, my two engineers came up with half a solution. They could fix the oven to work at a low temperature, allowing us to have our dinner at about 9 o'clock that evening, or we could go out to eat. We decided the latter was the better option.

I checked the local paper for restaurants that would have advertised as being open on Thanksgiving. We decided on the "Full Moon Saloon and Grill" in Luckenbach. When I called to make reservations, I was told they were pretty much filled up. But after I explained what had happened, they probably felt a little holiday spirit and said if we didn't mind a little crowding, they would be happy to seat us. "No," I said, we didn't mind.

The little crowding problem was taken good naturedly by the friendly Texas folks around us. It was almost like being at a big family dinner at a too-small dining room table. But after moving our chairs around to more space-effective positions, we were all comfortably seated.

We were not disappointed in the buffet dinner. Besides traditional turkey, we were treated to exotic-sounding entrées like Manicotti Florentine stuffed with Mushroom Duxelles garnished with two sauces, and Winter Squash Bisque with curry and toasted almonds, and much more, including a full dessert table.

On arriving back home, Dick again turned the oven on and through some engineering skills, was able to heat it to an acceptable temperature, and we continued to cook the turkey. When Bob was ready to leave, I handed him a cooler packed with yams, green beans, cranberry sauce, apple pie, and the rest of what was to have been our dinner that day. He decided he would pass on the turkey, and said he would pick up a rotisserie-cooked chicken at the supermarket to go with the trimmings for dinner on Friday, when his family returns.

The turkey was cooked to a beautiful, deep-golden brown when the meat thermometer registered as well done at about seven o'clock that evening. Gosh, it sure looked good, and we were looking forward to finally having or own homemade turkey dinner the next day.

The next morning, a nagging thought kept recurring to me. Maybe I should call the 1-800 turkey hotline and make sure the turkey is safe to eat. When I finally did call and told them the turkey had been cooking on and off, mostly on, for almost six hours, the best answer I could get was that it probably was safe, considering how long it was cooked. I didn't want to deal with the word probably, and I finally knew what I had to do. The turkey went into a plastic bag in the corner of the refrigerator to be put out on trash day. By now I could say good riddance.

TRISH BROWN SAVAGE

Forced Family Fun

GOOD OLD F^3: Forced Family Fun. It comes around three times a year for most families in this country: Thanksgiving, Christmas and Easter. That's all most families can stand!

When *my* clan gathers for yet another day of vigorous infighting, however, it takes a minimum of 12 months to recover—or forget—before agreeing to attend the next gathering for Forced Family Fun. We settled on Thanksgiving Day years ago, since—if you include in-laws and brief conversions—we count among our members born-again Christians, Orthodox *and* Black Muslims, Hasidic Jews, liberal Unitarians, uptight Episcopalians, Southern Baptists, carnivorous Buddhists, and nearly celibate Scientologists.

MOTHER: Welcome. Welcome all.
DAUGHTER-IN-LAW: You're *so* generous to host this Thanksgiving feast every year.
DAUGHTER: Yes, Mother, we *all* appreciate your holding the dinner here at the family farm.
M: Well, it's the only time I get to see all my grandchildren together.

Trish Savage escaped from Texas to obtain degrees from the University of Pennsylvania in Philadelphia. She wrote software for more years than she cares to admit. In retirement, she teaches GED math (no higher than fractions) and takes Dr. Matt Petti's creative writing courses at UDC.

D: And I get to see my favorite sister-in-law.

D-I-L: Thank you. We should get the cousins together more often. They barely know each other.

M: It's all a pleasure for me, a pure pleasure.

D-I-L: You're so sweet.

D: Oh, look. The kids scattered outside and the men are going into the den for the football game.

M: I guess it's a family tradition: women in the kitchen.

D: I'm just grateful we could all be here together.

D-I-L: What may I do to help?

M: Oh, don't bother yourself. Just go in and watch the game.

D-I-L: No, no. We want to stay here in the kitchen and help you.

D: Mother, you *never* let us help you.

M: Well, I think I've got everything under control.

D-I-L: Then maybe you should sit down and rest.

D: Oh, she'll never do that until the turkey is on the table. I know my mother.

D-I-L: I was wondering who's coming this year.

D: Don't ask.

M: Well, first there's Aunt Stella. She's upstairs resting.

D: Aunt Stella! Then Aunt Edith's not coming?

M: No, didn't you hear? Edith's resting in the arms of Jesus now.

D-I-L: I'm so sorry to hear that.

D: That explains why Aunt Stella agreed to come. Those sisters never could stand to be in the same room together.

M: Aunt Edith was the epitome of a proper, white, Southern lady.

D: The kids won't miss her. She reigned supreme for years, leaning forward like a gargoyle correcting their table manners.

D-I-L: *Some* of our children need that.

D: Good Episcopalian that she was, Aunt Edith'll surely come back from the grave if someone uses the wrong fork.

M: Well, now we're stuck with Aunt Stella, who was last sighted with a smile on her face in 1924.

D: Is *that* when her face cracked?

M: Yes, and it was pure *schadenfreude* when a neighbor's husband ran off with a stripper. But she *did* smile.

D: I'll have to take your word on that.

M: And then there's Uncle Horace.

D-I-L: I'm not sure I've ever met him.

D: Be thankful.

M: Just don't mention politics to Horace.

D: He's a rabid conservative, and listening to him talk about politics is like drinking from a firehose.

M: Now, now. Horace is a good Republican and a truly self-made man.

D: Let's hope he threw out the pattern.

D-I-L: Is Jimmy Earl coming?

M: Yes, and I'm optimistic that his wife's clothing will hide all her tattoos this year.

D: Hope triumphs over experience, once again.

M: I've been slaving over a hot stove for days.

D: Why don't you let me cook the giblets?

M: Heavens, no. Remember that year you forgot to turn off the heat? The giblets burned, the lid sealed shut, and the pan emitted a god-awful smell that permeated the house. Even the neighbors complained when I carried the pan outside to cool.

D-I-L: Maybe I should check on the kids.

M: I had to have the drapes and all my woolen clothes cleaned.

D: We'll eat when the football game ends, right?

M: Whatever chemical or gas that pan was putting out stung my eyes and irritated my throat. It was 25 degrees outside, but I had to sleep with all the windows open that night.

D: If I don't hide the remote, when this game ends the men will slide into another one.

M: I don't know why I always get stuck cooking the entire meal every year.

D-I-L: You told me last week on the telephone not to bring anything.

M: I did?

D: And I thought you'd never get around to deciding whether it would be lunch or dinner this year.

D-I-L: Yes, I was wondering all week myself.

M: Well, it's lunch. If my daughter and your no-good husband would just call their neglected mother once in awhile, I could tell them.

D-I-L: We don't have to come to your house *every* year.

D: I remember the drafts in this old house from my childhood.

M: Three sons. And no one ever calls me.

D-I-L: Our house has central heat.

M: How much effort does it take to lift the telephone receiver and dial a number?

D: I'm a basket case after three hours of driving with whiny kids.

M: Besides, in these days of speed dial, you can just push a single button.

D-I-L: You're talking to the *wrong* person. I call *my* parents.

M: We gather here because this house is the only one with a dining room table large enough for everyone.

D: We eat at *two* tables.

M: I've been slaving over a hot stove for days.

D: I *offered* to bring vegetables.

D-I-L: I offered to bring vegetables *and* a salad.

M: Where would we put them? Both the table and the buffet are full.

D-I-L: And you said you didn't need anyone to come early to help in the kitchen.

M: That didn't include time to set the table.

D: The table's already set.

M: Yes, I had to do that, too, myself.

D: Why did you use this dirty tablecloth?

M: It's not dirty, that's a cranberry stain. It's good luck to use that historic cranberry-stained tablecloth on Thanksgiving.

D: Yes, but you don't expect people to eat on it, do you?

M: What's wrong with it? Your great-grandfather paid $400 for it in Bangkok when he was in the Army.

D-I-L: I could have brought my famous sherry cake, but you said not to bring *anything*.

M: He had to bargain the price down from $1,200. You know how they are in Thailand.

D: There's a historic murky-dark smudge on the edge.

M: Great-grandfather was always good at haggling.
D: He was cheated if he paid more than $40 for it.
M: I remember it was stained at the family's 1937 Thanksgiving dinner.
D: I've seen better tablecloths in garage sales.
M: I just hope we can say a *Christian* grace this year.
D: Cleaner, too.
M: What a pleasure it is to have the whole family together once a year.
D-I-L: You might consider soaking the spot in lemon juice.
M: What! Subject a family heirloom to acid?
D: Or Goo-Be-Gone.
M: I've been slaving over a hot stove for days.
D-I-L: In my family, we always have oyster dressing.
M: Well, in *this* family, we never eat shellfish. It's somebody's tradition. I forget whose.
D: Why do you always scrimp on the stuffing?
M: Dressing is NOT the same thing as stuffing.
D: It *is* when you're stingy about the ingredients.
M: . . .
D-I-L: The men say they want to drag the TV set into the dining room.
M: Over my dead body.
D: Not a bad idea.
M: I'll bring out the turkey.
D-I-L: Wait, I don't smell anything. Shouldn't we smell the turkey cooking?
M: My God, we forgot to turn on the oven.
D and D-I-L, together: *We?*

SUZANNE FLUHR

Thankful for/on Thanksgiving

THANKSGIVING is my favorite holiday. Although many cultures have harvest festivals, Thanksgiving feels quintessentially, non-denominationally American. Americans of all religions, and of no religion, are thankful. We are thankful for our families and our friends. We are thankful our great-grandparents were brave enough to come here.

Of course, Thanksgiving does have some "issues." In elementary school, they teach us about the Pilgrims and Squanto, but no one warns us that Thanksgiving is sure to expose family pathology. Will I offend my sister who married Dizzy the Clown, if I ask her to tell her husband that I do not want the dinner devolving into a circus? Will my father start eating before everyone is seated? Will my husband's 97-year-old, Bulgaria-born grandmother refer to any ethnic group as peasants? Will my mother feel unloved if I ask her not to bring sweet potatoes with little marshmallows?

When I was a child, we used to pile into the family Chevy on Thanksgiving Day for the drive from our house in Philadelphia to

---

Suzanne Fluhr is a recovering lawyer who copes with her turkey-cooking phobia in Philadelphia, PA. In addition to still churning out the occasional legal brief, she has had personal essays published in the Philadelphia Inquirer *and the* Richmond Times-Dispatch. *She can be reached at JustOneBoomer@gmail.com.*

my grandparents' one-bedroom apartment in Brooklyn. In her tiny kitchen, Grandma Minnie would somehow produce a perfect, sit-down Thanksgiving dinner for 20. I have inherited her china, but not her confidence in the kitchen.

Despite my warm feelings for Thanksgiving, every year the prospect of cooking a turkey fills me with dread. The mere act of purchasing a turkey finds me transfixed in front of the supermarket turkey collection like a deer in the headlights. I have tried thinking of the turkey as just a big chicken, but the Thanksgiving turkey has assumed mythic proportions in my mind. I have nightmares about roasting the turkey for hours with hungry, expectant guests seated at the table in a Norman Rockwell tableau, only to discover that it is still raw at meal time. I have visions of my guests being admitted to the hospital with salmonella poisoning. I pour over cookbooks, surf Internet recipe sites, clip turkey-cooking tips from the newspaper, call my mother with inane questions, and keep the turkey hotline number near at hand. The fact that I have successfully produced a properly cooked Thanksgiving turkey for many years does not convince me that this won't be the year I fail miserably.

My turkey-cooking performance anxiety is accentuated because every year, we invite foreign students to share this most American of repasts with our family. My angst is therefore heightened by the thought that world opinion of the United States might somehow be influenced by the success or failure of my turkey-cooking efforts.

Our sons are always anxious to learn who will be joining us for Thanksgiving. One year we had our "Axis" Thanksgiving, with guests from Germany, Italy and Japan. When we shared our repast with a Serb, I didn't invite my Bosnian friend who had been granted political asylum in the United States. When Arnaud from France joined us in 2003, Freedom Fries were not on the menu. Last year it was a New Zealander and his Chinese girlfriend.

I'm always concerned when we invite Asians to join us for our Thanksgiving dinner, because despite the fact that they might happily consume jellyfish, ancient bird nests and shark fins, I've never come across turkey teriyaki or General Tso's turkey. I just tell them it tastes like—chicken (a big, probably too dry, too tough, tryptophan-laced, coma-inducing chicken).

One year, our sons listened with rapt attention to an imposing Sikh guest who explained that his turban held his hair that had never been cut. He was looking forward to the day his parents would arrange his marriage. And—oops—he was a vegetarian. Fortunately, there was plenty of string bean casserole—and sweet potatoes with little marshmallows.

If history is any guide, on the fourth Thursday in November, I will somehow rise above my turkey-cooking phobia. My husband will give a little speech about being thankful, and we'll say a prayer for those less fortunate than ourselves and for world peace. Our guests will be suitably impressed when the bird is presented. My husband will wield the carving knife and the juices will run clear. I will heave a sigh of relief.

Later, after the last of the pumpkin pie and whipped cream has been consumed and we have bidden our guests "adieu" or "sayonara" or "adios" or "auf wiedersehen" or "do vidjenja" or "zai jian," I will reconnoiter with the turkey carcass in the privacy of the kitchen. I'll take one last look for undercooked bones. I'll notice that there aren't many leftovers. And then, like an NFL wide receiver who just caught the ball and ran the length of the field for a touchdown, I'll point up towards heaven—and start washing the dishes.

ANGEL WILLIAMS

Post Thanksgiving 11/27/09

The obligation to socialize
Is once again before my eyes
I have to lie to be alone;
To avoid the constant ringing phone

No expense or pressure to cook for ten
No traffic to get somewhere and back again
I can make the things I like to eat
Which requires less time that I'm on my feet

I can watch old movies on TV
Cause there's nowhere that I have to be
The porch light's off so no one can see
How happy I am to be alone with me

If anyone knew my secret plan
They'd try to fix it as soon as they can
They'd invite me to join them wherever they go
I'd have to offend them by saying 'no'

They'd 'pop by' to see if I was all right
And ruin my plans for a silent night
When I reveal the truth the following day
They're upset that I chose to be that way

When I explain that I did what I wanted to do
They just can't believe that that would be true
You must spend Thanksgiving with someone or other
You must eat a meal cooked by somebody's Mother

This year I dodged the usual plan
Hoping my friends would understand
And forget what I did by the following year
So I can do it again without the usual fear.

Angel Williams majored in journalism and minored in public relations at Ohio State University. He currently lives in Los Angeles where he writes screenplays, novels, and children's stories.

ASHLEY DALTON FORSYTH

The Starving Gourmet

MOST PEOPLE end Thanksgiving dinner fat and happy. That is, of course, unless you're 12 years old, in an exclusive Chicago neighborhood, with a plate full of unrecognizable gourmet foods, and all you want is turkey. Thus was 1996.

My mother and her cousins, all single women in their late 40s, rotated Thanksgiving dinner each year among the suburbs of Detroit, Pittsburgh, and Chicago. The women are daughters of now-elderly sisters from Poland, and Thanksgiving became the one holiday that gathered the cousins. This time it was Sylvia's turn to host. Sylvia was the only cousin without children and with the most money. Sylvia's life was dedicated to her career, show dogs, polo ponies, rare wines and world travel. She didn't enjoy hosting and rarely offered to do so, preferring instead to come and go at her leisure without a holiday interfering with her agenda. The only other time that Sylvia hosted Thanksgiving, the meal was catered with "homemade" food.

In 1996, when Sylvia offered to host, the family was shocked and pleased. Anne, the youngest of the cousins, was going through a messy divorce, and fleeing Detroit with her three children was a

---

Ashley Dalton Forsyth was raised in Pittsburgh, PA, and received her BA in English Literature from St. Lawrence University in Canton, NY. She also earned a Masters Degree in Organizational Leadership from Point Park University in Pittsburgh, PA. She currently works in higher education in Philadelphia, Pennsylvania, and lives with her husband and pet rabbit.

welcome reprieve. My mom, the middle cousin, and I could travel easily—it had been just the two of us since I was seven, and the Michigan Avenue shopping on Black Friday was enough to lure us.

And so we packed up, got on the highway, and took off to Lincoln Park, Illinois. We all arrived in the waning hours of daylight, tired and hungry, but excited to see each other. I was the oldest in the next generation of cousins at 12. Josh, the only boy, was ten and already presenting as a hypochondriac who could easily shirk responsibility. Kaitlin was nine and constantly vying for the family's attention, but never could manage to steal it from Josh. Hannah had just turned six and enjoyed shrinking into the shadows of her siblings. We all grew up in upper-middle class families with more privilege than most. But Aunt Sylvia's house was filled with things we weren't allowed to touch: Ming vases, oriental rugs, and high-end Bordeaux. Before going to bed that night, my mom asked what time the caterers would arrive, and to everyone's amazement, Sylvia responded, "I'll be cooking. My last European excursion took me to Le Cordon Bleu for training; tomorrow's meal will be fabulous. Breakfast will be at 9 A.M."

The morning started off wonderfully, a beautiful display of fresh fruit and granola. We would have preferred Fruit Loops, but no one was complaining. The rest of the morning was quiet, filled with books and movies; lunch was served only a few hours later.

The lunch spread looked marvelous, but sadly didn't smell nearly as nice. Kaitlin was the first to speak up, "Honey, I shrunk the pickles!" This of course, in response to the very small gherkins that were neatly placed in a crystal dish with silver toothpicks. The cheese looked good but smelled terrible. The brown dip was no better. Sylvia then made the grave mistake of telling us that the brown dip was called pâté, and that pâté was French for duck liver. This sent Hannah into hysterics, and, I suspect, played a part in the fact that she became a Vegan after high school. We also learned that the mini Jell-O salad was, in fact, caviar. As a result of Hannah's meltdown, caviar was not explained to us that weekend, and we were led to believe that it was mini, yet foul-tasting Jell-O salad.

The afternoon seemed to drag—we were hungry and counting down the seconds until dinner. Five P.M. passed, 6 P.M. flew by, and around 7 P.M. we were restless, out of books, and driving everyone crazy. Sylvia had a strict closed-door policy on the kitchen, so we couldn't even speculate as to the meal's progress. My mom, known as the "cool aunt" to my younger cousins, decided to take us for a walk around the neighborhood. As we watched games of Turkey Day touch football wind to a close and saw people sitting in their panorama dining room windows, taking that last sip of coffee before the clean-up, my cousin Hannah, her big blue eyes welling with tears, looked up to my mom and said, "Aunt Marie, do you think if I knock on the door, they'll give me a turkey leg?" We returned to Aunt Sylvia's house even more excited for dinner. It was nearly 8 P.M., and we were famished.

Not long after our return did we hear those glorious words, "Dinner is Served." Trying to maintain order in our fancy holiday garb, we pushed and shoved to get to the table. We crawled onto the large, formal seats, took stock of the many utensils, fine linens, masterful centerpiece, and were ready for food.

First course, leek soup.

We slurped down the mint green goop as best we could, telling ourselves that turkey would follow soon. Second course, a bed of greens, topped with blue cheese and Dijon viniagrette. My cousin Josh, who perhaps due to his severe peanut allergy, had come to scrutinize all food, screamed, "Don't eat the cheese, it has gone bad!" Despite our strong suspicions that the cheese contained toxic mold, we were assured it was safe to eat. Sylvia insisted, "It's Stilton, for goodness sake." As if "Stilton," just like Penicillin, meant edible mold. Finally, the main dishes arrived, we watched with intense curiosity as each dish crossed the threshold into the dining room. We could smell the turkey leaving the kitchen—that glorious, Jack Daniels and sage-braised turkey.

They say that it can take years for the palate to mature; I can assure that it doesn't take place in the first 12. While a valiant effort, the souffléd yams, pancetta stuffing, gruyère mashed potatoes, and vinegar snap peas just didn't cut it. What happened to the green bean casserole, turkey skin you actually wanted to eat, and cranberry sauce shaped like a can? Kaitlin and Hannah started to whine; Josh and I, knowing better, sat and pushed around our food, secretly saying prayers that dessert would be the redeeming factor to this disappointing meal. Anne and my mom tried to persuade us to eat the delicious meal, while Sylvia, completely oblivious to our disappointment, raved that she had perfected the meal using her new culinary skills. Dessert was a pistachio gelato, which didn't look much different than the leek soup. The dinner ended with four hungry children, hundreds of dollars worth of leftovers, and was the most disappointing Thanksgiving ever.

Looking back years later, I would love to have that meal again. But as imagined, Sylvia never did host Thanksgiving until we were all in our 20s, and it was obviously catered. She always claimed it was because she wanted to spend time with the family instead of in the kitchen, but we suspect other intentions.

Black Friday on Michigan Avenue was spent as intended—complete with a family meal at McDonalds, Big Macs all around.

GERI TURNER

A Thanksgiving for Two

WELL, HERE IT WAS—Thanksgiving Day 2009. And I was alone. Alone, except for the challenge that had followed me through each of the last 28 days. How to get through the day without melting into a pile of salty tears from the hurt, fear, and loneliness that walked in and out of my heart and mind constantly.

I'd been out the day prior and picked up my "feast." That in itself had been a bit of a miracle, in that the entire meal plus a couple of necessities had only rung up at the local grocery store for just under $20. A good thing considering my life savings amounted to about $80 at this point. A Cornish hen, a broccoli crown, a tin of crescent rolls, and a baked potato were in my future. This menu had been a joking suggestion from my mother in the days prior. And there would be some for my canine companion as well, I'd determined.

Since I was staying at a friend's house since my arrival here 28 days ago, and since she had been in a fog of depression for most of the last nine months, and since she had travelled to Florida to be with

---

Geri Turner is a 46-year-old mother of one daughter. She recently relocated to Washington, DC, to be near her daughter, who currently resides with her father and step-mother in nearby McLean, VA. She can be reached at verbatim63@hotmail.com.

her family for the holiday, I had determined to spend the morning cleaning and straightening at least a portion of the house for her—and to keep myself busy. By 2:00, I had the dining room and living room completely dusted and the hardwood floors gleaming. A little rearranging of furnishings and placement of a few Christmas decorations, and I was feeling productive and hopeful.

A quick seasoning of the potato and the hen, and into the oven they went. Time to take a shower and answer some of the calls that had come in from well-wishers while I was in the cleaning frenzy. First one to my parents' home, where most of my siblings and their families were gathered for the feast of the day. All seemed satiated and relaxed after their meal, and each wished me an enjoyable rest of my day, expressing their wish that I had been there with them. Well, that plucked at that ever-so-sensitive heart of mine. But, nevermind. No need to wallow in things regretted that are not to be changed.

Second, to the absent roommate. They were just setting the table and awaiting other family members' arrival before dining on their own gobbler and trimmings. Got through that one okay. The kitchen was beginning to take on the aroma of a healthy meal on its way. A little Allison Kraus in the background and a glass of wine, and I was beginning to feel that it wasn't so bad to be situationally alone on this Thanksgiving holiday.

Last call, to my husband, 900 miles away in Louisiana. A deep breath and then dial. No, he wasn't going to celebrate Thanksgiving. It was just another day. He and his daughter would just get on the motorcycle and ride. As usual, I wondered why I had bothered at all. Maybe one day I'd just quit hitting my head against that brick wall and allow the wounds to heal themselves. Maybe one day soon.

Broccoli done, chicken and potato done, crescent rolls just about out. I set the table as if I had guests dining with me. Lit the taper candle and placed it in the center of the table. Dimmed the lights and bowed my head in prayer over my own repast. A heartfelt prayer flowing from my lips as I sat with bowed head and hands together, and the first tear fell onto my plate. I continued my prayers of thanks and blessings for all, and allowed the tears to flow freely. Get them out, I figured, then I won't choke on my meal.

It was just about then that I felt his presence. It was just about then that I heard him speak to me and thank me for having him at my table. And it was about then that I realized that I am never alone. The calm that came over me was never so welcome. The simple meal was delicious, and as I would later tell my mother, there was enough food to have fed two or three others. It was as if He had come and performed a smaller version of the miracle of the loaves and fishes I'd heard so many times in my life. I was satisfied, the dog had her bits of hen, and still there were leftovers.

I was grateful and reverent. I offered yet another prayer that if there was a hungry person somewhere near that could use what was left of my humble meal, that he would send them to my door, so that I might share with them not only the food, but the wonderful experience I'd had over my meal with Him. As it turned out, no one came to my door, but I determined that He knew that I was the one that would need those leftovers. After all, there was no other food in the house, and my funds were needed to last me at least another week.

I took a moment to reflect on how I'd secretly wished the night before, as I sat in church enjoying yet another beautiful Mass, that someone would just ask if anyone in the church didn't have a family to spend the holiday with, though I am not sure if I would have been humble enough to identify myself as one who would be alone, or if I was even brave enough to take someone's offer to come to their table.

A Thanksgiving like no other. A gift to have been alone with Him, without the chatter of idle conversation and TV noise in the background that is so much a part of these holidays. I will forever be grateful for being by myself and open to the visit, and I will never see Thanksgiving the way I did before November 26, 2009.

KRISTI PAXTON

Not Just Another Thanksgiving

I WAS BORN IN OTTUMWA IOWA, Thanksgiving Day, 1953. My brother tells me he painfully learned that year that you shouldn't mess with tradition. A precocious four-year-old only child, practically the center of the universe up to that point, he'd become accustomed to a certain level of service. But in 1953, apparently our mother failed to cook the standard holiday meal. She was preoccupied, giving birth to a little girl (me) who would rock my brother's universe and gradually withdraw him from the center, starting with the removal of his favorite Thanksgiving treat—pumpkin pie.

Our family learned from that holiday disaster, the sad story retold by my brother every year since. From that point we stuck with our traditions. Even after we grew up, never was there a Thanksgiving without home-baked turkey, stuffing, and pumpkin pie. Not until 2008 anyway, when our daughter, a college student in Brooklyn, announced she'd not be coming home for Thanksgiving. Since her holiday break was just four days long, she'd decided she didn't need the stress of long flights back to Iowa, making frantic connections in

---

Kristi Paxton was a postmaster for 22 years. Now a freelance writer, her weekly features appear in the Waterloo Cedar Falls Courier. *When not writing, she is a substitute teacher in Northeast Iowa. Kristi lives in the woods with her husband, Denny, and dogs, Bud and Ziggy. You can contact her at: kpaxcf@aol.com*

over-crowded holiday airports. She'd just stay in the dorms for her short break.

We did the only logical thing her mother, father, and older brother could do. We planned a trip to New York to spend Thanksgiving with Lauren there. Thoughts of Macy's Thanksgiving Day Parade danced like sugar plum fairies through my brain, and I just knew we'd be able to duplicate our family traditions a mere 1,111 miles east of our Iowa kitchen table. I could almost smell the turkey, thankful that a few lousy miles could not prevent our family from our cozy, Norman Rockwell-style gathering.

We were not disappointed. A New York Thanksgiving was all I had imagined and more... or less.

In the end, the trip didn't play out quite the way we'd planned. Nonetheless, we found much to be thankful for.

Not interested in The Plaza Hotel by Central Park (up to $4,500 per night), I did some dot com magic and found a posh "roomy" apartment we could sublet in the Financial District for a fraction of The Plaza's nightly fees. We were thankful it was an architect-owned, architect-decorated flat, in an historic building and surrounded by a decent neighborhood.

Alas, in New York, "roomy with two queen beds" translates to "one bed and a blow-up mattress crammed next to it on the floor," for anyone from out-of-state. We were thankful that it was oh, so... cozy. We were *really* thankful it included a tiny private reading room with a toilet. Wow!

When the airbed leaked, a simple push button made the loud, electric inflator do its magic. After long days of hiking city cement and climbing in and out of subway holes, we were thankful to be tired enough that most of us went back to sleep shortly after each noisy inflation. My family tells me that between inflations, a middle-aged woman snored loudly. I was thankful that I slept through it... every time! We were double-thankful that our architect-landlord took pity and dropped off a new airbed after only three fitful nights. We were even more thankful that the sink faucet dripped 24/7 just like ours in Iowa, making us feel right at home.

In the spirit of tradition, I had chosen our fabulous sublet for its full kitchen. I would cook some meals, allowing us to stretch our

Midwest middle-income budget, thus avoiding costly meals in overpriced city restaurants. I pictured an upscale Thanksgiving feast in our flat, with all of us gathered around the table depicted in its online photos. (In my sugarplum brain, the image was our exact table from home, magically transplanted from Iowa, but in a luxurious New York apartment overlooking sunsets on skyscrapers.)

But both online and sugarplum photography can be deceptive. Our skyline view was a sooty brick wall draped with some electrical wires. Our "full kitchen" was a dripping sink, cook top, baby oven and refrigerator in a neat row on a six-foot wall. In one easy motion, you could open the front door, remove your coat and knock a pan off the stove. With wall-to-wall beds, no counter and no actual table, I was thankful, therefore, to have an excuse not to cook many meals there. After all, where would I place the steaming, aromatic bird as I pulled it from the foot-square oven—on an unmade bed or on top of the refrigerator? I was thankful my Midwest soul was flexible enough to accept Plan B. We'd just deal with record-breaking parade crowds and find a cozy cafe with turkey and pie. The Visa bill would assault us later. For now, we had several days before Thanksgiving to search for a restaurant and enjoy New York. We decided to go with the flow and not look back.

Once we let go of our boring holiday traditions, the reasons to be thankful increased exponentially.

We were thankful to have several days on each side of Thanksgiving to enjoy what city life had to offer. And there was plenty, starting at our daughter's college in Brooklyn. She and her fellow dance majors performed while we were in New York, and we were thankful to get tickets to the show. My favorite part was a comedy piece where dancers dressed and moved like hypnotic 1950s housewives. I was thankful to be the loudest laugher there. (My family made certain I was aware of that fact.)

From college student entertainment, we moved on to Broadway. We were thankful to learn about a lottery for $26 tickets to "Young Frankenstein, the Musical." In a New York minute, the usher drew our names for front row seats. Maybe this doesn't sound worthy of a Thanksgiving prayer to you, but most Broadway tickets cost over $120 each. And the show provided more laughs to add to the ones we'd enjoyed at Lauren's show. By the time we got to Thanksgiving eve, we'd already tucked this holiday into our "Who's Who of Thanksgiving Memories." But there was more to come.

Legend has it that the best part of Macy's Thanksgiving Day Parade is the balloon character blow-up event at Central Park the evening before the parade. We met Lauren after her last class and loaded into the subway near our downtown apartment, with plenty of time to join the crowd that had assembled to steal our spots a good six hours prior. But by the time we headed the wrong way on the subway, got off and got back on heading north, we were late to our very important date. We totally missed seeing Spongebob Squarepants and the others take form in the shivering throngs of people around us. I think we saw the top of Mickey Mouse's left ear, but I'm not certain.

As we wove our way back through 16 million people all wishing they were someplace else, we didn't realize that by missing one event, we'd run into an even better one. (Which almost always happens in New York.)

As we gradually peeled out of the crowds, we stumbled upon a Thanksgiving miracle. A trendy antique (junk) store owner had decided to get rid of some of his inventory. There it sat, sparkling on the sidewalk, crowned with a "Free" sign. Free! My favorite word. Forgetting all about hot air Spongebob, we dug through books, furnishings, and strange artifacts sloughed from real lives of real New Yorkers. We were all thankful to have memorable loot to cart home. Among our treasures were two upholstered foam footstools for the dorm room, a large, cast cement letter "A" for our friend Allison, and a lovely picture book about the transvestites of New York City. We were thankful, indeed.

That night my sugarplum visions were replaced with dreams of a giant Spongebob, transvestites, and goofy housewives in misadventures involving missed subways and deflated parades. My crazy dream was another wonderful memory of our trip, and free as well! Who said New York had to be expensive?

We awoke Thanksgiving morning not unlike birds on migration day. Our strategy was to work our way north to the Macy's parade by staying on the west side of Manhattan as long as we could. We would get out of our subway near Times Square and weave our way east to the parade action. Thinking I was a genius, I'd rented the only cheap hotel room near there, hoping we'd camp out there the night before and guarantee a view. Since after looking at the room, nobody really wanted to stay in it, we used the lobby instead, lounging on its warm, shabby couches before, during, and after the parade. We went outside in shifts. Though I don't remember much about the parade itself, I remember sitting in that lobby, laughing, all of us shooting pictures of each other and the quirky, multi-faceted mirrored ceiling above us.

I would have been happy in that lobby long into the night. In fact, I might still be sitting there, but my family reminded me there was turkey to be eaten.

We settled on an East Village Texas barbeque—go figure—that in addition to turkey, baked beans, and hickory-smoked ribs, featured cornbread stuffing and margaritas. And someone delivered it to our sunny table on demand. How could that be wrong? Wait staff and margaritas were reason enough for me to toss aside any silly attachment to Norman Rockwell and dirty dishes.

After the actual Thanksgiving holiday, we had one more day in New York. Finding another $26 Broadway ticket lottery, this time for "Wicked," we held our breaths as the usher called other peoples' names. I'm thankful now that we lost. Skipping the show allowed us one last New York meal together. We found a warm Irish pub where dinner conversation eventually turned to family heritage. Our son, a political science student, asked about his ancestry. After a vague discussion including the words mutt, mongrel, and melting pot, our son pled his case, put it to a vote, and we unanimously decided to become Irish. Our family continues to be thankful that we chose a heritage with tasty food, cozy pubs, and lavish landscapes.

That last night we stayed up late to pack. We arose in the dark, wee morning hours to make our trip to the airport. But when I reached for the apartment door to head out, I learned we were hopelessly locked in. I was thankful my husband didn't explode. There we stood, single file, anxious and sweaty, wearing all the clothing that no longer fit into our bags, but frozen with fear of missing our flight. Thankfully, I had our architect-landlord's number on speed dial by that time. We were grateful she wasn't uptown at work. Within ten minutes, she appeared to let us out. We didn't hear an apology or an explanation. She should have been thankful we didn't yell at her.

As time separates us from that somewhat disappointing, but surprisingly memorable non-traditional Thanksgiving, I have no regrets. I've come to believe the human animal craves adventure and variety. In 35 years of perfectly predictable holidays, that unpredictable break with tradition in 2008 stands out like a big, beautiful sore thumb.

ZARA RAAB

Like Nothing Was Wrong

WHEN THE FAMILY GATHERED for Thanksgiving that year, they were pleased. They had not gathered around a well-laden table together in many years, not since the children—Jane, Ted, Eva—had grown up and gone their own ways. While Jane, Eva, their parents, spouses, and children waited for Ted to arrive, they talked and drank martinis. Jane and Eva's three teenage daughters were put to work tasting sauces, polishing a spoon suddenly found to have a tiny spot of tarnish, and setting the table.

In the midst of this hubbub, the front door opened, and there was Ted, disheveled, his clothes several sizes too large and spotted and stained, shuffling toward them for all the world like nothing was wrong. There was an awkward silence. Then Jane, ever the hostess, ushered them all to her ample table, set with her best china and all the traditional holiday foods. Oblivious to their surroundings, the teenagers dived in and generously sampled the fat, moist turkey, the baked yams, the stuffing of mushrooms and olives, cranberries, and each of the several kinds of fruit pies.

Zara Raab's poems have appeared (or will soon) in Poetry Flash, West Branch, Arts & Letters, Nimrod, Spoon River Poetry Review, *and elsewhere. Her* Book of Gretel *was published in spring 2010;* Swimming the Eel *will be published in 2011 from David Robert Books. She lives in San Francisco.*

Jane and Eva pretended to savor the sumptuous dishes, while in fact, holding back, afraid perhaps to awaken their own senses to the grit of disintegration. They ate determinedly, feeling the swift current of their own lives. It was not that they did not love their brother—they did—but neither sister knew what small, daily steps might be taken to help him. They had themselves experienced only large miracles—a good marriage, the births of healthy children, their husbands' successful careers.

At the table that Thanksgiving, there was laughter and, at one point, some raised voices when Eva forayed briefly into presidential politics, but the dinner on the whole went well. By eight o'clock, the bone china was packed into Jane's sleek European dishwasher, and the pots and pans had been put away, the leftovers neatly stored for another day. What leftovers they could not save, they threw away or gave to the dog. Even the younger set, normally rambunctious, felt overly full and ready for bed. Even so, they politely said their goodbyes, and Ted shuffled off as he had come—silent and ill-shod, complicit in the plan to save what could be saved, and for the moment, fed.

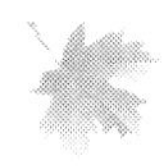

REBECCA J. LOVE

A Manly Sport

GETTING MARRIED and joining new family holiday traditions is never easy. In my case, easing my fiancé, Nicholas, into the family was even more of a challenge, as he is a female-to-male transsexual. Though it took some time and intense discussion, most of my family overcame their initial shock and prejudices. Nic's charming personality and easy humor was going to be a welcome addition around the holiday table.

Family and friends filled our home for the first Thanksgiving Nic and I spent together, creating the usual hectic and fun holiday atmosphere I anticipated each year. We'd been engaged for eleven months by then, living together in a small house. Though Nic survived his indoctrination into my family via birthdays and Mother's Day, he hadn't yet felt the full, frantic kitchen mania that Thanksgiving always evokes. The guest list that year included my mother and her boyfriend, my younger sister, Sara, my sister's long-term boyfriend, Nic's best friend, Barry, and a new acquaintance who didn't have another welcoming place for the holiday.

I began roasting the turkey in the early morning. A double batch of my famous apple, sausage, and cornbread stuffing quickly followed.

Rebecca J. Love lives in Arizona and works as a high school English teacher and librarian. She is madly in love with her culinary-impaired husband of six years and her adorable, four-year old son. Rebecca studies writing craft at Phoenix College in the Creative Writing Certificate Program.

I always have to make extra because people inevitably want to take some home to complement their leftover turkey. I barely had enough time to interrupt my frantically dusting and mopping fiancé for a kiss and to take a quick shower before my mother and sister came bustling through the door. Carrying a familiar, much-used wooden picnic basket crammed with food, my mother commandeered the kitchen.

Mum said, "You know, girls, this is the last Thanksgiving where the Swift women will do the cooking. Next year it will be the Love and Swift women. And if you ever get married, Sara, we won't have any name connections at all." My mother always valued her close relationship with her two daughters, and she worried that my forthcoming marriage might irreparably disrupt our family traditions.

Mum and Sara unpacked sweet and dill pickles, black and green olives, pickled okra, green beans, and watermelon rind for the relish tray. Fresh veggies in need of cleaning and steaming populated the countertops. Serving dishes, cutting boards, and utensils vied for space. Three women moved in a practiced, synchronized cooking waltz around the kitchen and into the dining room.

Nic escaped the flurry of kitchen activity to take his shower. He knew better than to get in the way of the Swift women when they were on a mission.

As savory sage and browned butter scents joined that of the nearly finished roast turkey, the other guests arrived. They snacked on the relish tray, stuffed mushrooms, crackers and cheese, nuts, and fresh fruit, while the final meal preparations were completed. I called Nic away from the appetizers for a moment to come into the kitchen.

"Could you take care of this?" I asked, handing him the carving set to sharpen and carry to the table.

"Sure. What do I need to do with this?" he asked.

I looked at Nic like he was from another planet. What do you do with a carving set? What was he talking about?

"The knife just needs a quick whetting, and then you carve the turkey when we bring it to the table," I said.

Nic's immediate look of horror startled me. He paled saying, "I don't know how to carve a turkey. I've never done that before!"

"You're the man of the house. You sit at the head of the table, and you carve the turkey," I said. I took it for granted that he knew what his role would be.

Then I couldn't help but laugh. I should have known. Nic's family didn't really do a big Thanksgiving like my family did. And when his family did get together for any kind of a more formal dinner, Nic's father or brother carved the meat. Nic's younger brother received the father and son meat-carving lessons, but Nic didn't. Growing up as a girl, he didn't merit that masculine kind of instruction.

Nic's countenance took on a look of grim determination. He grabbed the carving fork and knife, and he headed to the table. Nic cornered Barry in a quick, quiet consultation to glean Barry's few tidbits of manly carving advice.

At last, the moment arrived. Everyone gathered at the table, and as hostess, I carried the huge porcelain platter with the 20-pound turkey into the dining room. I placed the turkey, a domestic offering of many more gatherings to come, before my fiancé. Nic rose from his chair, grasped the cutlery with both hands, and approached the bird. His serious face studied the meat. He placed the knife, lifted it, and replaced it at what must have appeared to be a better carving angle. Then he erupted into laughter.

"I have no idea what I'm doing," Nic admitted. "Somebody please help me before I butcher our dinner."

Advice rang out from all corners of the table. Everyone laughed. Nic posed for an inaugural turkey-carving picture. Finally, he began to haphazardly carve the meat. It wasn't pretty—wedges of widely varying thickness, more ripping than slicing—but I have never had so much fun with this part of the Thanksgiving tradition.

Later that night, Nic and I chatted about the day as we continued to clean the kitchen.

Nic said, "You know, I realized today that being married to you, I will have many manhood tests. I never even thought about carving a turkey before as a skill I would need as a man."

"Yes, those traditional gender roles are everywhere, even in our own household," I agreed. "I just assumed you would know what to do, because that's what the men in my family have always done." I knew we would have to reconsider every gendered task and role we'd ever taken for granted from then on.

"You don't know what it means to be a man until someone hands you a knife," Nic laughed. "As long as you'll still kill the spiders, I'll figure out the other 'manly' things."

I smiled and said, "Ok. I'll buy some bug spray, and I'll get you an electric carving knife for next year."

STEPHANIE RUSSELL-KRAFT

The Quietest Day of the Year

I'VE ALWAYS KNOWN Thanksgiving to be one of the quietest days of the year. One year in middle school, I remember riding my bike down to my father's house after eating with my mom, and counting only three cars on the entire (and otherwise busy) two-mile ride down to his neighborhood. It was a silence I would have described as eerie, had I not known the circumstances. I considered the empty road, and smiled. It made me happy to know that the holiday was capable of slowing people down, if only for a day. But it also made me feel guilty, somehow, as if I had left the shelter of my home as a voyeuristic child, illicitly seeking the sights of the mid-day ghost town. The street was reserved only for cars taking last-minute shoppers to buy more wine or rolls.

"You're not supposed to be out here," the silence seemed to tell me, "go back to your family, take a nap, eat more."

"My parents are divorced," I wanted to reply, as I pedaled faster down the hill.

Stephanie Russell-Kraft, originally from San Diego, California, is a young writer living in the Lower East Side of Manhattan. She has published a number of pieces online, including many food and travel articles on the growing New York-based Web site womanaroundtown.com. She can be reached at srussellkraft@gmail.com.

I didn't think of that moment again until last Thanksgiving in New York, as I stepped out of my dorm at Columbia with my roommate, to buy a roasting pan for our turkey. We had gathered a modest crew of Californians and international students for the big day, and had plans to cook the entire meal in our suite.

Walking out of our building, I was struck by the silence of 114th Street. The block, which I was fortunate enough to call home for three years, was otherwise populated by overbooked Columbia students, fraternity boys, delivery trucks, and ambulances. It was only when living on the 12th floor of the adjacent building three years earlier, that I had been immune to the noise. On this morning, the roar of New York City had been reduced to a whisper, as if the only sounds being made were unintentional. I had rarely ever felt so calm so close to campus.

My roommate and I enjoyed the seemingly empty streets, not only on that Thursday, but for the rest of the weekend as well. We attributed the peace to the exodus of college students to their homes in the suburbs, and not to the holiday itself. For the first time in my undergraduate career (the only other was to be during spring break of that same year), I felt like I had time. With classes on break, and my social world out of town, I was free to spend three entire days with my roommate, working in the library, going to the gym, and watching TV. We were incredibly productive, and not only academically. We finished over ten movies, including the Lord of the Rings trilogy. If I had tried doing that at any other time during the semester, my thesis would not have been written.

But what was more striking than that bike ride, and the stillness on campus that fall, was my trip to the D.C.-bound bus on Thanksgiving morning in 2009. I woke up earlier than usual to finish packing my suitcase (and to watch an episode of "30 Rock") before deciding to take a cab to Chelsea, where the Bolt Bus was temporarily picking up passengers. And after carrying my bags down four flights of stairs, I exited the cage of 85 Pitt St. not to find the usual cast of characters chatting or drinking Colt 45s next to the stoop, but to an almost empty block, save one woman crossing the street nearly 20 feet away. Now I know the Lower East Side tends not to wake up early, but at 8 A.M. on a weekday, I expect to hear some noise. My roommate complains about the construction and yelling that starts at six every morning, and I'm never surprised to hear the newest Reggaeton beats blasting through our window from the cars passing below.

As I walked down Rivington St. this Thanksgiving morning, I could have sworn I heard the trees move. *The trees*. In New York.

I was worried that I wouldn't be able to find a cab, so I rushed down to Clinton St., dragging my suitcase and bag of Trader Joe's groceries with me. I had a taxi within seconds, though, and was soon making my way across Manhattan. As we continued on Houston, I couldn't help but stare out of the car window in fascination of the near-empty streets. I had never seen Lower Manhattan so deserted in the daylight, and suddenly noticed buildings I'd never thought to look at before. Heading into Chelsea, the expanse of 8th Avenue, a straight and massive road leading the way up to Central Park, stood out to me in an entirely new way. The sudden halt in skyscrapers at the park entrance actually looked like the edge of the world. The city had managed to slow down, and once again, I felt an odd guilt for watching it.

That evening, seated at the long and packed Thanksgiving table in my friend's Washington apartment, the silence still resonated with me. As we piled our plates with sweet potatoes and homemade cranberry chutney, I could not shake the effect of that taxi ride. I considered my surroundings and smiled. I was thankful not only for the good company I shared my meal with, but for the stillness of the streets that had reminded me how special the occasion truly was.

AMY STRINGER

Looking up at Turkey Day from Down Under

MY FIRST TIME CELEBRATING Thanksgiving was a while ago now, about five years I think, so to be honest, I can't remember exactly what happened or even who was present at the time. It's sort of blended in with other Thanksgiving days as the years have passed. So instead of attempting to retell a story of events that happened, I'm going to tell you what Turkey Day means to me as an outsider, as somebody looking at it with fresh eyes. I'm not promising any amazing insights, simply what I know to be true.

So I suppose it's one of those things: if you've done something for all of your life as far back as you can remember, you find it difficult to imagine doing it for the first time. I think that's because most people don't remember what the first year of their life was like.

It's like Vegemite, really.

What's that, you say? Vege what? Is that a legume? Do you eat it pickled? The thing is, Australians grow up eating Vegemite, which, for your information, is a salty, yeast-based spread, best served on

---

Amy Stringer followed her boyfriend to New Berlin, Wisconsin, originally at the beginning of 2005, and since 2009, has been living there full time. Before that, she grew up in Australia in Queensland and northern New South Wales, and lived in Sydney since she was 16.

warm toast over melting butter—so it's hard to imagine trying it for the first time, a real stretch of the imagination.

But we're talking about Thanksgiving here. By now you've probably realized that I am originally from Australia, "alanddownunda," as it's fondly named in that Men At Work song. And as an Australian, I've always been curious about Thanksgiving. My education on America growing up was mainly from *The Babysitter's Club* book series for teenage and pre-teen girls, and that television show in the early 1980s, *Degrassi Junior High*—wait! I've just been informed that show was actually Canadian. Oops. Like I said, my education on America was quite limited as I was growing up.

Anyhow, despite the fact that Americans average two or three fewer public holidays annually than Australians, I always feel they put a little more... effort into their holidays. A little more pizzazz, if you will. Especially here in the Midwest. Wisconsin to be exact. I attribute a large part of this to the fact that the winters here are usually well below freezing for a good chunk of the season. I'm talking about Christmas specifically, in terms of effort made, although Halloween can be pretty spectacular, too. When everything is covered in a blanket of white that sometimes sparkles in the sunlight, and sometimes looks dirty and downright doleful during cloudy periods, a few cheerful lights and maybe a larger than human-sized blow-up Grinch doll can inject just the right amount of warmth and color into the long, cold nights.

Back to Thanksgiving, however. I always remember how disturbed my fellow Australians and I were when we were presented for the first time with the completely bizarre notion of that most traditional of all Thanksgiving dishes... pumpkin pie. Yes, it seems absurd now, as it's one of my favorite desserts and definitely my favorite part of Thanksgiving dinner. But you have to understand, for my people, my Australian people that is, pumpkin usually comes in one of two forms: as part of a Sunday roast, or as a soup, neither of which is a staple food item in this country here. It was difficult at first to wrap our minds around the notion of pumpkin, usually enjoyed as a rich but savory vegetable on its own, or in blended soupy form, as the basis for a sweet dessert. And don't even get me started on what the heck we thought Cool Whip was. Cool what? Truthfully, I'm still not entirely sure.

I am a fan, though. Of Thanksgiving, that is. To me, it's like a precursor to Christmas. It's so similar. I mean, you get the overeating and drinking as the family comes together and bickers and laughs its way through the meal, followed by that overstuffed feeling of regret that sinks in later whilst you're tossing and turning and trying to sleep off the food and the angst. Seeing people that are "family" that you should be easy and familiar with, but when you only see them once or twice a year, what you wish would be natural and easy banter with one another is instead forced, awkward, and strange.

Don't get me wrong, the significance of the holiday hasn't passed me by entirely. I understand the weight it carries as a tradition that has deep roots in American history, which has, over time, delicately molded itself into meaningful celebrations held annually by millions of Americans country-wide.

I think the real reason that I like Thanksgiving is probably because it brings back memories. Strictly American memories. New, fresh, exciting experiences. Memories of first meeting my boyfriend's parents. Meeting all of my boyfriend's high school friends the night before Thanksgiving. Tasting that yam and marshmallowy dish that was homemade by his mother for the first time (there's another weird one). Attending my first Milwaukee Brewers game and tailgating for the first time (it just so happened that I went to my first game around Thanksgiving). Thanksgiving creeps up every year as the leaves are changing, decorating the skyline with flaming orange and sunburst yellows, and the first breath of winter approaches, providing relief from the hot summer months. All this I associate with this holiday.

It's fascinating to me also, because it is a purely American holiday that passes every year completely unacknowledged in Australia, unlike New Year's Eve or Christmas. We, too, have our own version of Independence Day (Australia Day), and even Halloween is beginning to be a fixture in my native country over the past decade.

On reflection, I think that Thanksgiving is more than just a precursor to Christmas. It is, historically, a celebration of the country by acknowledging the changing seasons and the changing times, as well as a gracious appreciation of the present. Even in the midst of those awkward family conversations, there is something to be said for the fact that every year, the effort is still made by so many families to get together and sit around the dinner table with each other, despite personal differences or ongoing personal or political events. Thanksgiving reminds me that I am in another country that, with all of its problems, still has the ability to take the time once a year to look back at the past, while peering into the future, and celebrating the present, and to do it all with grace, joy, and humility. It's pretty special, and I'm proud to be here and to be a part of it, pumpkin pie and all.

SAMANTHA C. HORROCKS

A Real Thanksgiving

FOODS FROM GREAT BRITAIN and Korea covered our table: eggrolls, shepherd's pie, kimchi, roast potatoes, overcooked carrots, peas, and cauliflower, steamed rice, bindaetteok, and sautéed shrimp with scallions. During our long tenure in the United States, this was our first Thanksgiving celebration. In a concession to tradition, our parents bought pumpkin pie. The multicultural buffet thrilled my brother, our friends, and me. Our parents co-hosted with bemused smiles. At the head of the table, you have our fathers: my dad from England and our friend's dad from Ireland. Their mother is Korean and our mother is Welsh.

"Can you pass the bindaetteok?" Jean asked me, pointing at the bean pancakes. I handed her the plate and said, "They are so tasty. Your mom totally has to teach my mom how to make them."

"They're not hard," their mom said.

"They're kind of strange Thanksgiving food, though," Jean's brother, Jonathan, said with a frown.

"At least it's Thanksgiving," my brother Matthew said. "It's just awesome we're celebrating, but I don't see why we couldn't have a turkey. You can never eat too much turkey."

Samantha Horrocks enjoyed a childhood of traveling throughout America. She is grateful that her father was not deployed, and that her friends' father returned safely. Matthew deployed to Iraq in November 2009. Samantha and her spouse live in Rochester, New York. They eat fish for Thanksgiving.

"We have turkey for Christmas," my mother interjected.

"We do have pumpkin pie," said their mother. "Everyone says that's a traditional dessert."

"Who made it?" Jean asked.

"The Commissary," her father, Kelly, answered, referring to the grocery store on the base. "I don't know how you get a pie out of a pumpkin."

"We've got a trifle, too," my Dad said.

"It's this strange but yummy custard, Jell-O, fruit thing," I told our friends.

Everywhere you looked, there were yellow ribbons in front of identical row houses on Ft. Eustis. The first Gulf War was in full swing, and we knew that our fathers might deploy before Christmas. Jonathan was in the fourth grade, one grade above Matthew and one below me. Jean was in first grade.

Everyone in our neighborhood was anxious that year. On drizzling fall mornings, we talked about the holidays while huddled beneath the bright yellow ribbon on the bus stop awning. Our need for celebration was intense. At school, civilian children muttered, "the war is just about oil."

I asked my mother about that and she said, "That's ridiculous. It's about defending Kuwait. People don't know what they're talking about. I guess they're not proud to be Americans."

Her response did not answer my larger question, "What is this war about?" The fear in her voice told me not to ask more questions. Her answers could not bring us comfort. Our culture provided pride and patriotism as guides; fear was not an option.

In early November, Matthew and I started talking about Thanksgiving to our friend, Jonathan. Many of our neighbors traveled to visit relatives. Only the Reid children and we did not have stories to share or family to visit. Jonathan asked Matthew and me what we did for Thanksgiving. After an awkward pause, we admitted that it was not a special day. Maybe Mom would get out the good china, but beyond that, it was just dinner. "They're from England," I explained to Jonathan. "I don't think they really know what to do."

"My parents are kind of like that, too. Dad's family doesn't really celebrate. They're from Ireland. And Mom's Korean, so I guess it's like they don't know what to do, either."

"Samantha and I keep telling them we need Thanksgiving, but Mom's all weird about turkey."

"She won't let us have it for Thanksgiving," I said as Jean edged into our secretive cluster. "It's like the holy food of Christmas or something."

"I just want a party," Jean said. "I don't care what we eat."

"Maybe you guys could come over," I suggested. "At least then it would seem like a real Thanksgiving. It's all about having family over, isn't it? Our dads are real good friends."

"I like that idea," Jonathan said. "Maybe if we let them make normal food, they'd go for it."

Turkey was the real reason we had never celebrated Thanksgiving. Holiday foods have a sacred quality to my parents. My parents love large roasts, but all the meat groups were taken up by other winter holidays. Boxing Day was pork or ham; New Year's Day was beef. Lamb was an option, but my Welsh mother was very particular about lamb. "You just can't get decent lamb in this country," was her lament. In her hometown, lamb comes fresh and tender from the neighbor's farm. My parents did not have qualms about Thanksgiving, but they had never seen reason to celebrate it before. It was foreign to their heritage, and our extended family resides in Britain, South Africa, and Australia.

Before the war, I don't think Matthew or I had considered ourselves to be American or British. We were dual citizen children. Americans told us we had funny accents. Our British family told us we had funny accents. In a childhood between two cultures, we followed the traditions our parents gave us. It was this year that we put up the cry to our naturalized parents that *we had to celebrate Thanksgiving*. Despite my parents' lackluster dealing with Thanksgiving in previous years, we demanded a *real Thanksgiving*. Having our friends' enthusiastic support helped. "We could invite the Reids over," we insisted. "They don't do much to celebrate, either. Maybe Yong would make some eggrolls." We knew that suggesting Korean food would entice our parents. They loved Yong's cooking, and we always enjoyed dinner at their house.

The British dishes were not unusual to Matthew and me, nor were the Korean dishes unusual to Jean and Jonathan. These were staple foods of our childhoods, and we spent enough time at each other's homes that nothing was a surprise. Yet, this was their advent as celebratory foods for us all.

"I think we should always have eggrolls for Thanksgiving," Matthew said. The importance of turkey dwindled as fast as the serving plates on our table. Eggrolls still remind me of Thanksgiving.

The celebration reassured us of our place in the many cultures of our lives. Gathering with the Reids made them family. This celebration was not just our parents humoring their adolescent children. They enjoyed this new holiday, too. We honored a myriad of traditions and hopes that day. We embraced abundance in the midst of our fears.

Two years later our family moved to Germany, and it was a decade before we saw the Reids again. When we saw them again it was the Fourth of July. We reminisced about our Thanksgivings and shared our stories of the past ten years. The American and British flags flew at our front door, and my Dad put a turkey on the barbeque rotisserie. July, it turns out, is far enough from Christmas to permit turkey.

I hold fast to the joy in that first Thanksgiving. It is a compelling reminder that we should give deep thanks for joy, friendship, and good food. Function is more important that form. Please pass the eggrolls.

FRAN ALEXANDER

Thanks for What?

IF CALENDARS were up to me, there would be no holidays from the last week of November to the first day of January. For all of its advertised joy, this can be an overwhelmingly oppressive time of year. From figuring out what to cook and whom to invite for Thanksgiving, to planning New Year's Eve out with friends or, dare I suggest, home alone, I am hard pressed to say I enjoy any of it. If you are one of those people who find this sad and shocking, no need to read on. But if you feel even just a tinge of recognition here, then you are in the right place.

My last Thanksgiving went from 16 people, the maximum I could fit in my dining room, to 27. No, make that 28, because one guest's girlfriend was added at the last minute. Of course, I could hardly say no, but I was assured that she was so tiny that she wouldn't take up any room. Since I pride myself in allowing my guests to sit in chairs, I said she would have to squeeze in anyway. However, I was truly happy for her on the tiny status.

The seating spread into the hallway, despite promising my children that we would all be at one table together, and I was saddled

---

Fran Alexander is a freelance writer in NY's Westchester County, currently pursuing an MA in Writing at Manhattanville College. Her articles on women's health, education, parenting, and art have appeared in NYMetroParents publications, Inside Chappaqua *and several newsletters. She's a board member of Chappaqua Summer Scholarship Program for inner-city students.*

with the challenge of making it feel more like an honor than a punishment to be dispatched to the table in Siberia. I also had to renege on serving family-style, since the large crowd dictated a buffet instead. How could I make up for these transgressions after my kids had traveled from near and far to be with us? My solution was to delegate, or should I say abdicate, seating assignments to them and thereby throw all special requests to the wind. If Aunt Helen had to sit next to her ex-husband's cousin, who may have stolen from the family business, at least it would not be my fault.

On to the menu. I debated between one large turkey and two smaller ones. Before I go on, I have to mention that I do not like cooking large animals, and even a smaller turkey qualifies as an oversized creature for me to be handling in the kitchen. I would much prefer birds already cut up by a butcher, thus twice removed from their original state. As for the necks and the gizzards that so many cooks cherish for gravy makings, they could easily find their way into my garbage can, but alas, I go along with the turkey-cooking ritual.

I elected to go with the two smaller birds after a great deal of thought, for several very good reasons: shorter cooking time, lower chances of a turkey-lifting-induced hernia, and more drumsticks for all the cavemen. My fresh, organic, free-range, grass-fed, antibiotic-free, pastured, and sustainably farmed turkeys (my urban agriculturalist daughter insisted) arrived frozen, despite being ordered early per the butcher's instructions. When I brought them home in the box he packed so nicely for me, they hit the counter like a sack of rocks, and I called him in a dither. He insisted the turkeys were really fresh and not frozen—it was just too cold in the truck where they were stored overnight in the freezing weather. Unacceptable, I said, I have to start preparing them now. They're just hard on the outside, he insisted, run them under warm water for a half-hour. Ugh. I would rather have used my supermarket coupon for an enormous, free, frozen turkey, even if it was shot up with hormones and who knows what else. I countered, how about I find other fresh turkeys and return these? Okay, he conceded, he'd been having trouble with his customers all morning about this. After several phone calls, I found another butcher with some fresh, organic, free-range, grass-fed, antibiotic-free, pastured, and sustainably farmed turkeys, drove an hour back and forth to pick them up and return the frozen birds, and finally rolled up my sleeves.

At last, hours later, the cooked birds rested on the counter, waiting to be carved by my brother, the ex-caterer, and master carver. The oven was now open for heating up all the sweet potato and stuffing-glop varieties that my most generous and helpful guests had brought. There were mounds of mashed sweet potato with marshmallows, pineapple, maple syrup, nuts and cinnamon, and vats of mushy bread stuffing with chestnuts, sausage, mushrooms and yes, even spinach and raisins.

Have I mentioned that I don't even really like this whole meal in the first place? By the time everyone piles all the side dishes onto their plates with the turkey and gravy, it's a heap of slop, nothing resembling the feasts of those glossy magazines or the Food Network, with their beauty shots of glistening, hairsprayed meals. And since crowd control was overlooked, when the meal was finally announced, my guests made a mad dash for the serving trays. Before I knew it, the food had been inhaled by the inebriated diners, some of whom were already going for seconds, just as I finally sat down with my own plate. With barely an opportunity to even take a moment for prayer and thanks, I'd like to know thanks for *what* anyway, for I have now modified this holiday name to Thanks-But-No-Thanksgiving. (Talk to my lawyer if you plan on using that.)

After three days of preparing, ten minutes of eating, and two days of cleaning up, take a deep breath. It's time for Chanukah, Christmas, Kwanzaa and the New Year. Perhaps you're wondering if you have to celebrate with the same people you've just fed for Thanks-But-No-Thanksgiving (TBNT). Or maybe you're hoping to get invited somewhere else instead, so you can relax into guest mode, like your grown children do when they come home for the holidays. Not yet quite grown up, these children are just grown in size (although some may still be tiny as we have already learned), and they have come home to be mothered, not to be mother's helpers.

Lest you think I'm all Scrooge and no heart, there were some moments of love and laughter during our celebration. I did bring together some relatives who had drifted apart. One cousin, at long last, shared his mother's secret brownie recipe—"break up chocolate and add sugar, flour and eggs." My daughters were thrilled to meet a quasi-relative who had been in the Peace Corps after college (more ammunition for their argument against nine-to-five desk jobs). And my clean-up time was happily spent with my father-in-law's second wife, who can always be counted on to enjoy a little gossip.

Finally, we ended the evening piled onto the couches in the den, watching old family movies of our three daughters dancing, playing, eating, and laughing together. Proof of a happy childhood for one searching grown child who seemed to have somehow forgotten about that. There she was on the screen for all to see—an ebullient, giggling, somewhat bossy, little girl. And for that, I do give thanks.

Made in the USA
Lexington, KY
28 October 2010